# THEOLOGY OF THE BODY IN ONE HOUR

Totus Tuus
PRESS
2017

JASON EVERT

Theology of the Body In One Hour
Jason Evert
© 2017 Totus Tuus Press, LLC.

Unless otherwise noted, Scripture quotations are taken from *Man and Woman He
Created Them: A Theology of the Body*, trans. Michael Waldstein (Boston: Pauline Books
and Media, 2006). All other Scripture quotations are taken from the Revised Standard
Version: Catholic Edition (RSVCE) of the Bible, copyright © 1996 by the Division of
Christian Education of the National Council of Churches of Christ in the United States of
America. All rights reserved.

If any copyrighted materials have been inadvertently used in this work without proper
credit being given in one manner or another, please notify the publisher in writing so
that future printings of this work may be corrected accordingly.

Nihil Obstat: I have concluded that the materials presented in this work are free of
doctrinal and moral errors.                                                        ,
+Rev. Michael L. Diskin
November 6, 2017

Imprimatur: In accord with 1983 CIC 827 § 3, permission to publish this work is hereby
granted.
+Thomas J. Olmsted
Bishop of Phoenix
November 6, 2017

Published by Totus Tuus Press, LLC.
P.O. Box 5065
Scottsdale, AZ, 85261
www.totustuuspress.com

Cover by Devin Schadt
Interior by Russell Graphic Design
Printed in the United States of America
978-1-944578-84-8
978-1-944578-85-5 eBook
Library of Congress Control Number: 2017913005

# CONTENTS

# ACKNOWLEDGMENTS

I am deeply grateful to Dr. Michael Waldstein, Christopher West, Dr. John Grabowski, Damon Owens, Bill Donaghy, and Katrina Zeno. Thank you not only for reviewing this book and offering your insightful recommendations and improvements, but also for your many years of prayerful study of the Theology of the Body. Your devoted work in unpacking the Holy Father's wisdom has been a blessing to me, and was essential in the creation of this work. Most especially, thank you for living the Theology of the Body. You are a gift to the Church.

# PREFACE

Before retiring to bed on a Tuesday night in the Vatican, Saint John Paul II prayed the Liturgy of the Hours, meditating upon the following words from Saint Peter: "Stay sober and alert. Your opponent the devil is prowling like a roaring lion looking for someone to devour."[1]

Long after others in the papal apartment were asleep, a noise awoke his secretary, Monsignor Stanisław Dziwisz, who left his room to investigate. His room was adjacent to the Holy Father's, but he noticed that the sounds were not coming from the Pope's room, but from his chapel. Although late-night prayer was not uncommon for John Paul, Dziwisz peered in to be certain that everything was all right.

The sight was typical: John Paul immersed in contemplation alone before the tabernacle. The Pope usually spoke to God with very simple words, and often prayed during adoration like Jesus did in Gethsemane, talking with his Father.[2] This night, Dziwisz noticed that John Paul indeed seemed troubled. The disturbance he overheard was the Pope speaking aloud to God, asking repeatedly, *"Dlaczego? Dlaczego?"* ("Why? Why?"). Out of reverence, the monsignor backed away from the chapel and returned to his room for the night.

John Paul celebrated Mass the next morning, but was unusually reserved during breakfast afterward.

The Pope's typical jovial and engaging demeanor toward the sisters and guests was subdued. Instead of asking questions and conversing about an endless variety of topics, he was recollected and withdrawn. He ate no breakfast, and drank a cup of tea.[3]

That afternoon would be an important one: During his Wednesday audience, John Paul was preparing to announce the establishment of two ministries in the Church that would address the problems facing families in the modern world.[4] One of these, the Pontifical Institute for Studies on Marriage and the Family, would become the main teaching arm of the Theology of the Body.[5]

On his way to deliver his message, the Holy Father rode in the Popemobile across Saint Peter's Square. As he was blessing children and greeting the crowds, gunshots from a Turkish assassin rang out. An ambulance rushed the Pope in his bloodstained cassock to the hospital, where he narrowly escaped death.

Had God given him a premonition of his suffering the night before? The answer to that question will likely remain a mystery known only to John Paul.

Was there a link between his suffering and his efforts to build up marriage and the family? This he affirmed, saying, "Perhaps there was a need for that blood to be spilled in Saint Peter's Square."[6] He added, "Precisely because the family is threatened, the family is being attacked. So the Pope must be attacked. The Pope must suffer, so that the world may see that there is a higher gospel, as it were, the gospel of suffering, by which the future is prepared, the third millennium of families. . . ."[7]

After recovering from his wounds, John Paul returned to the Vatican and resumed his proclamation of God's plan for human love: the Theology of the Body.

# INTRODUCTION

While camping at the World Youth Day vigil in Kraków, I spoke with a young woman who was preparing to enter her first year of college at a prestigious university in California. She pulled her phone out of her backpack and showed me where her online college application required her to check the appropriate box to indicate her gender.

There were eighteen boxes to choose from.

I read through the litany of genders, and noticed that two were missing: male and female. (Facebook—which invites its users to identify as one of more than fifty genders—at least offers them the possibility of choosing to be male or female.) The university application, however, did allow the incoming students to choose "cis-male" or "cis-female," which means that the biological sex one was "assigned" at birth aligns with the gender one chooses for one's identity.

While some seek to expand upon the number of genders and create a spectrum of options, the ultimate goal of gender theory is not diversity. After all, diversity requires objective differences. The goal is to erase the sexual difference, and thus to eliminate the meaning of the body.

Where is this coming from? The Second Vatican Council prophesied our culture's sexual identity crisis by stating, "When God is forgotten . . . the creature itself grows unintelligible."[1] Although the Theology of the Body was written before many of the modern ideas of gender theory became popular, it was ahead of its time in offering a clear answer for them—and for many other key issues about sexuality and the body.

## What is the Theology of the Body?

The Theology of the Body is the popular title given to 135 reflections written by Saint John Paul II. As a cardinal in Poland, he (Karol Wojtyła) planned to publish them as a book titled *Man and Woman He Created Them*.[2] Before this could happen, he was elected pope, and instead delivered the content in 129 Wednesday Audiences during the first five years of his pontificate.

The thousands of vacationers and pilgrims who gathered to see the Holy Father at these audiences had no idea that the Pope's biographer would later describe the Theology of the Body as a "theological time bomb set to go off, with dramatic consequences, sometime in the third millennium of the Church."[3]

What could be so explosive about a Polish bishop's theological reflections on the body?

To answer this, consider how the human body has been viewed throughout history. Thousands of years ago, Gnostics and Platonists believed that a person's true self was different from his or her body. One Gnostic sect, the Manicheans, believed that man's destiny was to set his spiritual essence free from the pollution of matter. Because the body was material, it was not only inferior, but evil. In fact, it was considered a sin for a woman to give birth because she was bringing more matter into existence! Centuries later, puritanism considered the body to be a threat to one's soul. Meanwhile, the philosopher René Descartes proposed that the soul is like a ghost trapped in a machine.

All these views about the body have one element of truth in common: Our bodies and souls aren't in harmony. However, the body is not unimportant compared to the soul. Nor is the body something we "have," or something that encumbers our soul. We are our bodies, and our bodies reveal us. However, our current state is not the way God created us in the beginning. The discord that exists within man is the result of original sin.[4]

While some individuals devalued the body and cared only for the soul, others fell into the opposite mistake. Atheists and materialist philosophers argued that the human person is nothing more than his or her body: There is no soul, and the body has no meaning.

Although these ideas might seem like debates reserved for philosophers and theologians, consider what happens when entire cultures accept these misguided notions of what it means to be human. If man has a body but no spiritual dimension, what distinguishes him from other animals? Why should he act differently or be treated differently? On the other hand, if a person's true identity is found in his spirit alone, then man's view of himself becomes uprooted from any objective reality. Truth would then be defined by a person's feelings. As a result, masculinity and femininity would be viewed as social constructs, not realities created by God. But if masculinity and femininity don't exist, then what becomes of marriage and the family?

Because there has been so much confusion about the meaning of the human body, John Paul set out to present a total vision of man that would include man's origin, history, and destiny. Instead of arguing from the outside in, offering people a litany of rules, he invited them to seek the truth about reality by reflecting on their own human experience. The writings of Saint John of the Cross played a key role in shaping John Paul's style of thinking. His philosophical studies on of Max Scheler and other phenomenologists further sharpened his ability to observe human experience. John Paul doesn't begin by explaining what man ought to do, but by explaining who man is. In the Pope's mind, people will know how to live if they know who they are.

It has been said that rules without a relationship creates rebellion. This is true with parents and children, and it's especially true with the relationship between God and humanity. John Paul knew that laws don't change hearts. When people view morality as a rigid list of imposed regulations, they might temporarily behave themselves out of guilt or fear, but they often abandon the faith. The Pope understood the futility of this approach, and knew that a fresh re-presentation of the Church's teachings on sexual ethics was overdue.

What the modern world needed was not just a defense of the Church's teachings, but rather an unveiling of God's original plan for the beauty of human love. Culture needed something that wasn't simply intellectually convincing or morally upright, but rather something that corresponded to the deepest yearnings of the human heart.

Unfortunately, many have grown deaf to these yearnings and hear only the urges of the body. But no matter how numb one might be to the deepest aspirations of the soul, everyone can relate to the ache of solitude, the experience of shame, and the desire for communion. In the Theology of the Body, John Paul explored these experiences and more, to reveal how God's plan for humanity is stamped not only into our hearts, but also into our bodies.

When people discover the Theology of the Body, they often exclaim that they've never heard anything like it before. This is because many people learned about sexuality in a religious framework that focused only on what is forbidden and permitted. Others learned about it through the lens of modern sex education, which reduces one's sexuality to biology and sensuality. This might count as "sex ed," but it's not a true education in human sexuality.[5]

Properly speaking, "sex" is not something people do. Sex is who we are as male and female persons. The Theology of the Body reminds us of this broader meaning and offers compelling answers to questions such as: Who am I? What does it mean to be human? How should I live? It delves into delicate questions regarding marriage and sexual ethics, but does so while inviting people to rediscover the meaning of life. Through it, one realizes that modern man's sexual confusion is not caused because the world glorifies sexuality, but because the world fails to see its glory.

For those who have disregarded the Church's teaching on human sexuality because it seems out of touch with the modern world, the Theology of the Body offers a fresh perspective. Its insights are not pious reflections offered by a theologian who was isolated from the daily struggles of married life. On the contrary, they are the result of decades of personal interactions between a remarkable saint and the countless young adults and married couples that he accompanied through their vocations. These couples attest that although John Paul had a great ability to preach, he had an even greater ability to listen.

The Theology of the Body comes from the heart of a saint who listened intently not only to others but also to the God who could provide meaning to their lives. He was no stranger to suffering, living under Nazi and Communist regimes and having lost his family by the age of twenty. While such trials might lead some to abandon their faith, John Paul's was forged by them, as he sought answers to the deepest questions about life's meaning.

John Paul also possessed a staggering intellect, and according to his secretary, spent three hours each day reading.[6] Although he was dedicated to the intellectual life, John Paul's prayer life took priority. His colleagues attest that he seemed to be continually absorbed in prayer, as can be seen from the fact that he considered the busy Paris Metro to be "a superb place for contemplation."[7]

His greatest devotion, however, was to the Blessed Sacrament. He never omitted his Holy Hour on Thursdays, even while traveling internationally. If the organizers of his trips didn't make room for it in his schedule, he would make time and simply arrive an hour late to their program. When his assistants attempted to convince him to decrease the amount of time spent in this devotion, he refused, saying, "No, it keeps me."[8] He knew that apostolic mission derives its strength from life in God.[9] It is from this man's heart, mind, and soul that the Church has been given a tremendous gift: the Theology of the Body.

### Structure

The Theology of the Body is comprised of two parts. The first focuses on three passages from Scripture, or "words" of Christ. In it, John Paul examined the dialogue between Jesus and the Pharisees regarding marriage and divorce.[10] Then he reflects upon the words of Christ from the Sermon on the Mount, in particular those concerning committing adultery in one's heart.[11] Finally, he turns to Christ's words regarding the resurrection of the body.[12] By means of these reflections, he explains the redemption of the body. If fact, in his final catechesis, he describes the content of the whole work as "the redemption of the body and the sacramentality of marriage."[13]

The Theology of the Body is thoroughly biblical—as can be seen by the fact that the Pope draws from forty-six books and more than a thousand Scripture citations. However, among all of the passages he quotes, the three mentioned above are his focus. He compares them to the panels of a triptych, which is a work of sacred art consisting of three panels, or parts. When the three images are displayed together, they present a fuller understanding of a topic of theology (in this case, the human person).

The three parts of John Paul's triptych are original, historical, and eschatological man. Original man is who God created man to be in the beginning, before the dawn of sin. Historical man refers to the current state of humanity, burdened by original sin but redeemed by Christ. "Eschatological" has its roots in the Greek word for "end," *eschaton*, and refers to the glorified state of man in heaven. Together, these three epochs of human history form what John Paul called an "adequate anthropology"—an understanding of what it means to be a human person.

In the first part of the Theology of the Body, John Paul used the above three "words" of Christ to explain man's call to live out "the spousal meaning of the body." This phrase is the heart of the Theology of the

Body. It means that the human body has "*the power to express love: precisely that love in which the human person becomes a gift* and—through this gift—fulfills the very meaning of his being and existence."[14] (This gift of self can be expressed not only through marriage, but also through celibacy for the kingdom of God.)

In the second part of the Theology of the Body, the Pope analyzed "The Sacrament" which is the "great sign" of Christ's love for the Church and the love between a husband and wife. He explained what the gift of self means in terms of the "language of the body," and how men and women are called to live it out, especially as it relates to building their families.

～

Those who have read the 500-plus pages of the Theology of the Body will attest that it is not an easy read. In fact, the 128-page introduction to the book could probably use its own introduction![15] Because of its dense philosophy and theology, it interested only scholars for decades after it was written. Thankfully, a groundswell of enthusiasm about the riches contained within it has begun to spread within the Church. Academics and lay evangelists are mining its depths and sharing its jewels with the faithful. Many excellent books have been written for this purpose, and many more are sure to come. The purpose of this brief introduction is not to replace them, but to whet the appetite of the reader not only to read them, but to accept the invitation of John Paul:

Those who seek the fulfillment of their own human and Christian vocation in marriage are called first of all to make of this "theology of the body" . . . the content of their lives and behavior. In fact, on the road of this vocation, how indispensable is a deepened consciousness of the meaning of the body in its masculinity and femininity![16]

Condensing five years of papal audiences into a sixty-minute summary is ambitious, to say the least. Although the following six chapters of this book are brief enough to blaze through in one hour, do not rush. The insights of John Paul are profound, beautiful, and life changing, but sometimes difficult to grasp. They are meant to be savored, meditated upon, and integrated into our lives. Just as a fine glass of wine can be consumed in seconds, its richness is only appreciated by the person who savors every drop. The same can be said of the Pope's wisdom. Saint Francis de Sales taught that "Haste kills all devotion,"[17] and the Theology of the Body deserves devoted study. Throughout this text, you will notice hundreds of endnotes that will lead you to the original sources of the Pope's thought, should you wish to explore his teaching more deeply. Take your time absorbing the fruits of this man's contemplation. He was a world-class philosopher, a gifted theologian, and most important, a tremendous saint.

# PART 1

# THE WORDS
# OF CHRIST

1

# CHRIST APPEALS
# TO THE "BEGINNING"

**Original Man**

When most people think about the book of Genesis, they dismiss it as an assortment of ancient and unscientific fables that belong in a children's coloring book. As a result, they assume that the texts have little to offer modern man.

Although the creation accounts in Genesis are pre-scientific and archaic, it would be a mistake to consider them to be unscientific or outdated. In Genesis, God did not intend to present a scientific treatise, but to express profound truths about humanity that are just as valid and unchanging (and archaic) as the laws of physics.

A person who attempts to scientifically debunk Genesis could be compared to an optometrist who reads the Song of Songs and then uses a retinoscope to prove that the eyes of the woman are not doves, nor are they pools of Heshbon, despite the claims made by her lover. However accurate the doctor's findings may be, they don't invalidate or disprove what the lover sees in his bride. Likewise, the truths found in Genesis do not contradict science. Rather, they delve into a realm of truth that lies beyond the reach of material science.

Therefore, when the Pharisees questioned Jesus about divorce, he led them back to the beginning, to the Creator's own words regarding his plan for human love. The Gospel of Matthew recounts the exchange:

> Some Pharisees came to him to test him and asked him, "Is it lawful for a man to divorce his wife for any reason?" And he answered them, "Have you not read that from the beginning *the Creator created them male and female* and said, '*For this reason a man will leave his father and his mother and unite with his wife, and the two will be one flesh*'? So it is that they are no longer two, but one flesh. Therefore, what God has joined let man not separate." They objected, "Why then did Moses order to give her a certificate of divorce and send her away?" Jesus answered, "Because of the hardness of your heart Moses allowed you to divorce your wives, *but from the beginning it was not so*." (Matt. 19:3–8)

In order to give the Pharisees an adequate answer about marriage, Jesus knew that they first needed to have what John Paul called an "integral vision of man," rather than a partial or fractured one. Unfortunately, our only experience of humanity is the sinfulness that we have inherited. But this isn't the whole picture of man. Jesus leads his listeners back to Genesis in order to take us beyond our limited understanding.

It is easy to prove that we lack this integral vision. For example, if you were to say that the book of Genesis explains the story of "Original . . . ," what word would you use to fill in the blank?

"Sin."

While this is true, John Paul pointed out that the story of creation also reveals what humanity, or original man, looked like prior to sin. It reveals his experience of original solitude, original unity, and original nakedness. Understanding these concepts is the basis of understanding what it means to be human. When they are revealed, we see the beauty of the first panel of John Paul's triptych.

### Original Solitude

From the beginning, the body of Adam revealed that he was alone in the world: "It is not good that the man should be alone" (Gen. 2:18). He wasn't alone simply in the sense that he lacked Eve. Indeed, his body revealed that he was created for another, and her absence was felt. But even after her creation, man stands alone before God.

The human body reveals that man is alone among all earthly creatures as a person. Unlike the animals, he is not an irrational beast, driven purely by instinct. He is a subject: a person with a conscience who is aware of himself and is capable of self-determination. Therefore, Adam's solitude is first a reference to his uniqueness as a person within creation.

When God declared that it is not good that man should be alone, he revealed a profound truth about man: Our essence is not fully realized in aloneness. We realize it by existing with someone and for someone.[1] Our original solitude is fulfilled by becoming a gift. Because we have free will, we can make a gift of ourselves to others in many ways, and in particular through our vocations. As John Paul noted, young people "know that their life has meaning to the extent that it becomes a free gift for others."[2]

However, the most fundamental "other" that we have been created to give ourselves to is God. We must first fill our ache for communion with God before we fill it with humans. Otherwise, a relationship can become an idol, and all idols are meant to be broken. This isn't because God is envious. It's because no creature can fulfill the ultimate desire of a being that is created for infinite bliss. This is why C.S. Lewis remarked that idols eventually break the hearts of their worshippers.[3] Without God, no matter how many companions a person may have, he or she remains alone.

God desires to be our first love not simply because he knows that nothing else will satisfy us, but because he wants us to become what we are: creatures made in the image and likeness of love. As Pope Benedict XVI wrote, "It is therefore the vocation to love that makes the human person an authentic image of God: man and woman come to resemble God to the extent that they become loving people."[4]

**Original Unity**

In the beginning, God "made them male and female." As mentioned above, Adam's body revealed his uniqueness as a person. However, it also demonstrated his aloneness. Even before Adam saw the first woman, he could have sensed that creation was incomplete.

If you consider every system within the human body (circulatory, nervous, digestive, and so on), you will notice that all but one of them function without the other sex. Only the reproductive system requires a member of the other sex in order for it to serve its purpose. The male and female bodies are made for each other.

Therefore, when Adam first sees the body of Eve, he gasps that she "is bone of my bones and flesh of my flesh" (Gen. 2:23). Or, as John Paul explained, "He seems to say, *Look, a body that expresses the 'person'!*"[5] Adam expresses wonder, admiration, and fascination. He is captivated by the person she is, which is revealed in and through her body. John Paul noted, "*Love unleashes a special experience of the beautiful,* which focuses on what is visible, although at the same time it involves the entire person."[6]

After creating man and woman, God gives mankind His first command: "Be fruitful and multiply, fill the earth" (Gen. 1:28). But why? Why did God endow mankind with the ability to procreate? Angels don't have this ability. Why should man? Some presume that mankind would cease to exist otherwise. But this isn't true. God could create an endless supply of humans if he so desired. But, he desired for man to be a reflection of his creative power, through which he expresses love. Genesis 1:27 states, "Let *us* make man in *our* image, in *our* likeness."[7] What does this mean?

Love cannot exist in isolation. There must be a lover, a beloved, and a fire of love between them. This is the Blessed Trinity: a communion of Persons in life-giving love. God created man in his image and likeness, and this means that in our bodies, we make visible the invisible mystery of God: He is love. As the *Catechism of the Catholic Church* states, "God's very being is love. By sending his only Son and the Spirit of Love in the fullness of time, God has revealed his innermost secret: God himself is an eternal exchange of love, Father, Son and Holy Spirit, and he then has destined us to share in that exchange."[8]

We resemble God not simply because we have an immortal soul, an intellect, and a free will. The sexual complementarity of the male and female bodies, in their masculinity and femininity, reveals that we are made for relationship, for a communion of persons. The same cannot be said of any other creature. Although plants and animals are capable of reproduction, they cannot make a gift of themselves in love. A communion of persons is only created by a mutual gift, and this requires free will—not just a biological instinct to reproduce.

John Paul explained, "Man becomes an image of God not so much in the moment of solitude as in the moment of communion. . . . [This] constitutes perhaps the deepest theological aspect of everything one can say about man."[9]

Pause and absorb what John Paul is teaching. He's proposing that the sexual intimacy shared between a husband and wife is an icon of the inner life of the Trinity.[10] In saying this, he is not sexualizing heaven, but is revealing that our sexuality points us there when it is properly understood. The call to be fruitful and multiply is a call to live in the divine image: to make a gift of ourselves through life-giving love.

The call to communion that is revealed in the body is a sign of what persons are supposed to do: make a gift of themselves to others and ultimately to God, in the image of the Trinity. Obviously, there are countless ways to make a gift of oneself that are nonsexual. For example, each work of mercy (feeding the hungry, caring for the sick) is a form of life-giving love. Through this gift of self, we love like God, and by doing so, fulfill our destiny.

Before original sin, Adam and Eve enjoyed original unity. They lived in harmony with God, with each other, with themselves, and with the rest of creation. With sin came division in all four forms. Original sin not only ruptured the union between humanity and God, it also wounded our unity with others, within ourselves, and with all of creation.

Although God intended the sexual differences between men and women to be a gift that would unite them through complementarity, sexual differences after the fall often divide them and become an obstacle in their personal relationships. In order to eliminate this struggle, modern culture sometimes attacks gender as if it were the problem. In other words, "The real problem is the rigid social constructs that perpetuate the myth that men and women are different. If we eliminate sexual differences, the problem will be solved." But it is precisely our differences that make union possible. Without difference, there can be no complementarity.

The male/female difference cannot be reduced to societal influences or even to body parts and chromosomes. In fact, our sexual differences are only shown in a limited measure on the outside.[11] It is who we are as persons, down to our souls.[12] Those who are in heaven now might not have their glorified bodies yet, but they remain male and female. Likewise, after the resurrection of the dead we will regain our bodies in their masculinity and femininity.[13]

Contrary to what gender theorists propose, sex is not something "assigned at birth" that might be at odds with one's true identity. Our body reveals our identity! One's sex is a gift bestowed by the Creator at the moment of conception.

All of this may sound like hate speech or bigotry to those who might identify as a gender that does not correspond with his or her sex. Proponents of gender theory have done an excellent job of marketing the idea that a person's true identity is not determined by one's body. Although they claim to assist individuals in embracing their identity, they're only giving people permission to reject it. It is the Church that encourages individuals to embrace the deepest truth about their identity, revealed through the body, even if this process of discovery is a difficult one.

But why should a person's identity depend upon his or her body? Why did John Paul say that our sex is not only decisive for our bodily individuality, but that it defines our identity?[14]

Imagine if someone struck you, and you asked him, "Why did you hit me?" and he then replied, "I didn't hit you. I hit your body." Odds are, you would not be convinced or consoled by his bad anthropology. You are not separate from your body. You don't just "have" a body. Your body is you. It expresses the person and reveals the soul.[15]

In fact, the human body is the only creation of God that makes a person visible. Angels are personal beings, but they don't have bodies. Animals have bodies, but they don't reveal a person. This is why John Paul said that the body is a "sacrament" of the person. A sacrament is a visible sign of an invisible reality. In one of the most important passages of the Theology of the Body, he explained, "The body, in fact, and only the body, is capable of making visible what is invisible: the spiritual and the divine. It has been created to transfer into the visible reality of the world the mystery hidden from eternity in God, and thus to be a sign of it."[16]

This is why, as he explained in his *Letter to Families*, "The body can never be reduced to mere matter: it is a *spiritualized body*."[17] It is not created to be molded, manipulated, or mutilated.[18] Nor are masculinity and femininity cultural inventions. They are ordered to an end, namely spousal union and parenthood.[19]

Our bodies are not meaningless. As Cardinal Christoph Schönborn wrote, "The beauty is real and reliable. Its light can be traced back to God's original guiding intention for man and woman."[20] The "fundamental fact" of human existence is that we are made male and female, and therefore our sexual identity is not something we define, but something we receive.[21]

While this may seem obvious to some, for others it poses a great challenge. Some feel alienated from their biological sex, or attracted to members of the same sex. To pretend otherwise would feel disingenuous to them. How can the Theology of the Body offer them anything but a rigid and binary dismissal of their experiences? How can people who experience gender dysphoria or same-sex attractions express their true identity according to God's design while remaining authentic to their interior feelings?

Although this topic is too complex to sufficiently explore within the scope of this work, three considerations could be offered as an introductory answer:

First, unfair gender stereotypes sometimes cause individuals to question their identity. Pope Francis noted, "Such rigidity, in turn, can hinder the development of an individual's abilities, to the point of leading him or her to think, for example, that it is not really masculine to cultivate art or dance, or not very feminine to exercise leadership."[22] But the solution here isn't to eliminate gender, but to avoid overaccentuations of it. He added, "I ask myself, if the so-called gender theory is not, at the same time, an expression of frustration and resignation, which seeks to cancel out sexual difference because it no longer knows how to deal with it. Yes, we risk taking a step backward. The removal of difference in fact creates a problem, not a solution."[23]

A second point to remember is that the deepest truth of a person's identity is that he or she is a beloved son or daughter of God. If we detach ourselves from this reality, we often define ourselves by lesser things, such as our attractions, occupations, virtues, or vices. But because our behavior flows from our identity, it is essential that we remember that each person is made in the image and likeness of God, and is therefore called to make a gift of himself or herself. Only by living according to this truth, stamped into our bodies, will we find true fulfillment. As Cardinal Raymond Burke explained, "The twofold expression of the human person is not heterosexuality and homosexuality, but male and female. This is the authentic theology of anthropology: that God created man: 'male and female he created them.'"[24]

Finally, it also helps to keep in mind that original sin disrupted not only the unity between men and women, but also the unity within each person. John Paul pointed out that this "brings with it an almost constitutive *difficulty in identifying oneself with one's own body*."[25] Although he was not directly addressing the question of gender dysphoria in this passage, the fact remains that each person, in his or her own way, experiences a division between the body and soul. Speaking of Adam after the fall, John Paul continued, "It is as if he had experienced a specific *fracture of the personal integrity of his own body, particularly in that which determines its sexuality* and which is directly linked with the call to that unity in which man and woman 'will be one flesh' (Gen. 2:24)."[26]

This fracture manifests itself in a variety of ways. As mentioned above, some overspiritualize their identity and disregard their body. Others do the opposite. Everyone wrestles to some extent with what it means to be male or female. The Pope explained, "The *Creator has assigned the body to man as a task, the body in its masculinity and femininity*."[27] Man has been given a task to rediscover his dignity and calling, and this call is revealed in and through the body.

The Church is not afraid to invite people to be introspective about their sexuality, nor is the Church asking that individuals be dishonest about their feelings. However, sometimes it's necessary to peel away layers of woundedness to arrive at one's calling. To discover God's plan for each person, we are called to look to Christ, who "fully reveals man to man himself and makes his supreme calling clear."[28]

To some, this may feel like a simplistic solution to a complex personal issue. But the heart of the matter is trust: Do we trust that God has created us good, and that he doesn't make mistakes? Do we trust that in making each person male or female that he wanted to reveal something to us that would ultimately lead us back to him? If we erase the complementarity of our sexual difference, we eliminate what it reveals: that we are created to make a gift of ourselves in imitation of the God who created us.

In the beginning, the original unity that Adam and Eve experienced in marriage was a clear sign of something that pointed beyond them. This is why John Paul called marriage the "primordial sacrament."[29] Marriage was created to be *the* sign of his love for humanity and his plan for our lives. It would also make visible the invisible mystery of God himself—that he is love. Although this sign was obscured because of original sin, it has been revealed once again in Christ.

Understanding original unity is essential to understanding the Theology of the Body because it reveals who God is (a life-giving communion of persons), who we are (made in his image), and how we are to live in time and in eternity (by making a gift of ourselves to others and to God).

## Original Nakedness

It has been said that the deepest desire of the human heart is to see and be seen in love. In the beginning, Adam and Eve experienced this in a unique way. They were naked without shame, created in what John Paul called a state of original innocence and original nakedness. Some presume their lack of shame indicates that they were naïve, like small children, or primitive in their understanding, like an isolated jungle tribe. But this is not the kind of innocence to which John Paul is referring.

In the beginning, sin had not yet clouded the human heart. Therefore, the original innocence of Adam and Eve was the special grace of holiness, which is a participation in the inner life of God.[30] This holiness enabled them to see themselves and one another as God sees them. They were conscious of the meaning of their bodies and how it revealed their call to love. This purity of heart enabled them to see each other as a gift to be received, not as an object to be grasped.

In his book *Love and Responsibility*, Karol Wojtyła taught that the person is a good toward which the only proper attitude is love.[31] Because of his or her value, a person can never be used as a mere means to an end. For Adam and Eve, this value was clear. Therefore, their lack of shame indicates not a lack of awareness, but a fullness of understanding of the meaning of the body.[32] Adam and Eve felt no shame because there was no need for it. The naked body of the other was not a distraction from that person's value, but rather a clear revelation of it.

Unfortunately, there is a widespread myth that the original sin of Adam and Eve was sexual intimacy. This has never been the teaching of the Church. In fact, it was before the fall that God commanded Adam and Eve to be fruitful and multiply. Not only is sexual intimacy not inherently sinful, Adam and Eve would have experienced sexual desire in a completely pure way. The idea of pure sexual desire might sound like a contradiction to modern man because society mistakenly thinks of sexual intimacy itself as impure. But in the beginning, it was not so.

John Paul explained that before sin clouded their vision, in their nakedness, Adam and Eve would have seen one another through the very "mystery of creation."[33] This is the mystery that God is love, he creates out of love, and calls man and woman to love.[34]

Because of this, the original couple would have looked at each other with the "peace of the interior gaze."[35] Women, in particular, perceive when they are being viewed merely as an object for another person's gratification. When a woman senses lust in the heart of a man, she feels a restless vulnerability and even resentment. One expert on the female brain noted that a woman's sexual pleasure is greatest "only if the amygdala—the fear and anxiety center of the brain— has been deactivated."[36] Eve would have no need for a defensive attitude toward her body or heart because

Adam had the ability to view her with the most intense and pure love possible.

John Paul explained that it was this capacity to see one another "with all the peace of the interior gaze, which creates precisely the fullness of the intimacy of persons."[37] Affirmation of the person makes the authentic communion of persons possible. How could there be a true union between two people if they are unaware of the magnitude of the gift of the other?

Adam and Eve understood the magnitude of the gift. Their original innocence enabled them to see original nakedness as the human body's capacity to image God as love. This original nakedness without shame is precisely the key to understanding the Theology of the Body. In fact, John Paul proposed that their nakedness without shame revealed the holiness of God in the visible world.[38] Needless to say, the last thing that people think nakedness reveals is holiness. But that is only because they don't understand the meaning of the body.

### The Spousal Meaning of the Body

In one of the most important passages in the Theology of the Body, John Paul explained the "spousal meaning of the body." This means that the human body has "the power to express the love by which the human person becomes a gift, thus fulfilling the deep meaning of his or her being and existence."[39] The spousal meaning of the body is "the spiritual beauty of the sign constituted by the human body in its masculinity and femininity."[40]

In John Paul's eyes, the spousal meaning of the body is *the* fundamental truth about human beings.[41] To understand what it means to be human, one must understand this.

Because people are made in the image and likeness of God—and God is love—this means that people are made in the image and likeness of love. They are created to make a gift of themselves. The Church declares: "This likeness reveals that man, who is the only creature on earth which God willed for itself, cannot fully find himself except through a sincere gift of himself."[42] This truth about man is stamped into every person's body, because in its masculinity and femininity, the body is oriented to the communion of persons.[43]

In the Gospel of Matthew, Jesus asked, "Have you not read that from the beginning the Creator created them male and female and said, 'For this reason a man will leave his father and his mother and unite with his wife, and the two will be one flesh'?"

But why did Jesus say "For this reason?" What's the reason?

The union of the man and woman points to something beyond themselves. When a man and a woman live out God's plan for love in their bodies, they make visible the invisible love of God. If a person is looking for the meaning of life, it is closer than he or she might think. It's stamped into every person's sexuality as male or female: to love like God by making a gift of one's self.

In the beginning, man experienced original happiness because of the discovery of the spousal meaning of the body.[44] Because of original innocence, Adam and Eve were free to love as God created them to love. Unlike the animals, their sexuality was not ruled by instinct, but was personal. They possessed what John Paul called the "freedom of the gift" because they had mastery over themselves.[45]

This freedom is the foundation of the spousal meaning of the body. Without it, spousal love, which is a love of total self-donation, cannot exist. After all, a person cannot give what he or she does not have. If a person does not have self-control, it becomes impossible to make a gift of one's self. Instead of making a gift of one's self, the person uses another as an outlet for one's perceived sexual "needs."

However, through self-mastery a person becomes free to love. In fact, it could be said that to love with a pure heart is to rediscover the meaning of life.[46] Purity empowers men and women to experience a taste of the "beatifying beginning" when Adam and Eve were naked without shame.[47]

Contrary to what many have come to believe, purity does not involve having a negative attitude toward sexuality. In fact, the opposite is true, because only the pure in heart are able to understand its greatness. Our bodies reveal that we're not simply called to make a gift of ourselves to others, but ultimately to make a gift of ourselves to God in this life, and in the next.[48] When the sexual act is divorced from the spousal meaning of the body, it is robbed of its depth. But when it is understood in light of God's original design, it points to mankind's deepest desire, which is infinite love.

2

# CHRIST APPEALS TO
# THE HUMAN HEART

**Historical Man**

In the first part of his reflections, John Paul focused on God's original plan for humanity. In the next cycle, he turned his attention to a second "word" of Christ, delivered during the Sermon on the Mount. With this passage, he begins to examine "historical man":

> You have heard that it was said, "You shall not commit adultery." But I say to you: Whoever looks at a woman to desire her [in a reductive way] has already committed adultery with her *in his heart*. (Matt. 5:27–28)

There is no shortage of "hard sayings" in the New Testament, and this is without question one of them. Although these words of Christ might seem discouraging or impossible, John Paul asked, "Should we *fear* the severity of these words or rather *have confidence* in their salvific content, in their power?"[1]

What is it about these words that John Paul found so hopeful? To most, they sound like a condemnation.

Although we cannot return to a state of original innocence, God does not command that which cannot be done. Therefore, Jesus' admonition against adultery in the heart shows that purity is possible and realistic.[2] The reason why we think otherwise is that we sometimes become so attached to our sinful habits that we normalize our brokenness and gradually identify with it. We assume lust is "natural," sin is "human," and God "made us this way." As a result, many believe that the Church is out of touch with reality by expecting anything different from humanity. But if we question the power of redemption, we're the ones disconnected from the reality of what it means to be made in the image and likeness of God.

In the words of the *Catechism*, "Jesus came to restore creation to the purity of its origins."[3] All too often, the Christian message is reduced to the forgiveness of sins. As wonderful as this is, redemption is more than the cancellation of the debt of sin. Our bodies and our desires are in need of redemption, too. Although the redemption of the body won't be complete until the end of time, it begins now. though the spousal meaning of the body has been threatened, it has not been suffocated.[4] Christ came so that it might be rediscovered.

It bears repeating that the human body did not become evil because of original sin. In fact, John Paul argued that the body and sexuality remain a value not sufficiently appreciated.[5] Whereas concupiscence limits, violates, and deforms the meaning of the body, purity of heart opens our eyes to it.[6] This is why Christ appeals to the heart. He knows where the battle will be won or lost.

### The Fall

The harmony that once existed between man and God, man and creation, men and women, and man's body and soul was unfortunately short-lived. John Paul explained that the serpent invited man to doubt the heart of God, to disbelieve that he created man out of love.[7] Instead of seeing love as the motivation behind creation, God is viewed as a tyrant and a holdout. As the Pope explained in his book *Crossing the Threshold of Hope*, original sin attempts to "abolish fatherhood."[8] Man cast the Father out of his heart.[9] With the fall, the period of historical man begins.

As John Paul rightly remarked, original sin "is not an isolated event at the dawn of history."[10] Although some people consider the story of original sin to be a religious myth, no other doctrine of Christianity is easier to prove. One needs only to watch the nightly news to see that humanity is yoked with weakened wills, disordered appetites, and darkened intellects. This inclination to sin is called concupiscence. It is what constantly pushes one to cross the boundary between passively experiencing temptation and actively choosing it.[11]

Because of original sin, man does not rule over his body with the same ease as original man, with simplicity and naturalness.[12] In the beginning, man's desires were ordered rightly because the body and soul were in harmony. Man didn't struggle to obtain dominion over bodily desires. But because of concupiscence, the interior freedom of the gift was lost. As John Paul pointed out, the beauty of the male and female body, as an expression of the spirit, is obscured.[13] What flows from this is that the subjectivity of the person gives way to the objectivity of the body.[14] *"The relationship of the gift changes into a relationship of appropriation."*[15] Giving shifts to taking. Donation degrades to possession.[16] Therefore, according to John Paul, the root of sexual concupiscence lies in casting suspicion on the Gift, in turning one's back on the Father. Sin originates in our spirit, not our flesh.

## The Entrance of Shame

After the fall, Adam and Eve hid themselves from God (and each other), sewing fig leaves together to conceal their nakedness. Many people assume that they felt some sort of embarrassment or insecurity about their bodies. But the shame they experienced was not due to a realization that something was wrong with their bodies. Their bodies remained "very good."

What wasn't good was that they had lost the peace of the interior gaze. The simplicity and purity of Adam and Eve's original experience was shattered.[17] Through sin, they forfeited the clarity of vision that original innocence offered them. This is why they felt a need to conceal their bodies. In particular, they veiled the parts of their bodies that determined their femininity and masculinity.[18]

This lack of trust between them showed that their unity had been compromised.[19] John Paul explained: "The words of Genesis 3:10, 'I was afraid, because I am naked, and I hid myself,' confirm the collapse of the original acceptance of the body as a sign of the person in the visible world."[20] Although their sexuality—as male and female—originally revealed their call for union, it became an obstacle in their personal relationship.[21] John Paul continued, "The diversity, or the difference between the male and female sexes, was abruptly sensed and understood as an element of the mutual opposition of persons."[22]

Every person seeks to be affirmed in his or her full value, but without original innocence, the person recoils. The sexual values that once had revealed the truth of the person are now concealed in order to guard the value of the person. This is why the Pope rightly observed that they were not so much ashamed of the body as they were ashamed of concupiscence.[23] In order to understand John Paul's thought, it is necessary to understand this deeper dimension of sexual shame.

### Healthy Shame

When most people think of shame, they equate it with unhealthy guilt. If guilt tells a person, "I did something bad," shame tells him or her, "I *am* bad because of what I did." This unhealthy shame is not what John Paul has in mind. Rather, shame understood within the context of the Theology of the Body is a tendency to conceal the sexual values sufficiently to prevent them from eclipsing the value of the person, thus opening a way toward love.[24] Because it is rooted in the dignity of the person, when it recognizes a threat to the value, it preserves the value in an interior way.[25] Therefore, John Paul sees shame as a natural way to discover the value of the person.[26] Although shame distances man from woman, at the same time it creates the suitable basis for them to approach one another on a personal level.[27] In other words, it sets the rules for the communion of persons.[28]

In the beginning, man and woman were immune to shame as a result of their love and the fact that they were conscious of the meaning of the body.[29] John Paul considers this to be "*the distinctive character of original innocence*"—it enabled man to see the spousal meaning of the body.[30] Original innocence excludes the need for shame at its very root. Although such purity of heart might seem to be a distant notion to modern man, an echo of original innocence remains in us today—in who we are and who we are made to be for each other.[31]

## Modesty as the Guardian of Love
When the concept of "modesty" is mentioned in today's culture—particularly on secular college campuses—any hope of rational dialogue is drowned out by accusations that those who promote modesty are "slut shaming" and advocating "rape culture" by failing to

be "body positive." There is anaphylactic reaction to the word, as if modesty required a woman's rights to be rolled back to the Middle Ages. But John Paul displayed a sensitive understanding of why the term often ignites such a volatile reaction.

Throughout history, people have blamed the body—particularly of the woman—as the cause of lust. The woman is seen as the seductress, the occasion of sin. But in John Paul's mind, lust is a problem of the heart, not the body. Blaming the body for lust is a loophole to avoid the true issue: our hearts.[32]

If every woman clothed herself from head to toe, lust would remain. Put differently, a thief does not become a philanthropist when jewels are locked away. The cause of theft is not the jewels in the window of the store but the greed in the heart of the robber.

Consider why police sometimes place "bait cars" in high-crime areas. They leave the keys in the ignition of a vacant and unlocked car and put valuable items inside to draw attention to it. People who feel no need to steal walk past the vehicle without difficulty. But those who are inclined to commit larceny often seize upon the opportunity and end up in jail . . . only to blame the police for "setting them up."

It is the same with the body. Only a mistaken idea of modesty transfers the evil of lust to its object. In human sexuality, the object of desire isn't evil. In fact, the Pope pointed out that "victory must go hand in hand with an effort to discover the authentic value of the object."[33] This is one reason why it is so counterproductive to shift the blame of lust to the body; by doing so, a person robs the body of its simple and pure meaning.[34]

The body isn't the problem. If anything, it's the answer! In fact, one Orthodox scholar noted, "Beauty is the only thing that can make the eye chaste."[35] After all, virtue can only be gained by love of the good, not by merely warding off evil. What's needed is not for the body to be permanently veiled, but for its meaning to be unveiled, so that the glory of God can be seen in the body. What's needed is the transformation of the deepest movements within the human heart.

This is not to say that people ought to wear whatever they wish, without regard for the weakness of others. In fact, modesty plays an essential role in transforming the hearts of those who are inclined toward lust. This is because modesty is an invitation to contemplation. It is a reminder that a person's body is not public property, nor is it the best thing a person has to offer the world. Rather, the body is an invitation to love. But this spousal meaning of the body needs to be protected from concupiscence, and that is the purpose of modesty.

This isn't merely a woman's job. In fact, modesty isn't the exclusive duty of females any more than lust is the exclusive problem of males. It is the heart of the human person—male and female—that is in need of redemption.

## The Heart of Man

In his reflections on historical man, not only did John Paul reiterate Christ's words about adultery in the heart, he mentions adultery nearly two hundred times in this one cycle of teachings, gradually going deeper every week! But why the insistence, and why was Jesus so concerned about what happens only in the heart, rather than with what actually happens in the body?

Jesus is obsessed with the heart because whoever wins the heart (love or lust, God or the devil) wins the mind, the eyes, the body, and the soul . . . for eternity. Actions flow from the heart and one's destiny is forged through one's actions. Jesus is obsessed with the heart because that is where we know and live the spousal meaning of the body. What's at stake is the meaning of life: living in God's image and likeness.[36]

The human heart has become "a battlefield between love and concupiscence."[37] The more concupiscence dominates the heart, the less we experience the spousal meaning of the body and the less sensitive we become to the other as a gift.[38] We begin to see others as objects to be used instead of persons to be loved, and we lose sight of the fact that others are created for their own sake, not for ours.[39]

The way one person looks upon another matters, because the look expresses what is in the heart. We reveal by our looks who we are.[40] In his letter on the dignity and vocation of women, John Paul stated: "Each man must look within himself to see whether she who was entrusted to him as a sister in humanity, as a spouse, has not become in his heart an object of adultery."[41]

The Pope acknowledged that Christ's words on adultery in the heart are severe, and they require us to assess our interior acts, motives, and impulses.[42] He explained, "The inner man is *called by Christ to reach a more mature and complete evaluation that allows him to distinguish and judge the various movements of his own heart.* One should add that this task *can* be carried out and that it is truly worthy of man."[43]

Although Christ's words about adultery in the heart are demanding, they are not a condemnation but a calling. His words are not only a task but a gift. By restating Christ's words, the Pope was reminding the Church in the midst of our brokenness, addictions, and weakened wills, that our call to love runs deeper than our urge to use. No matter how weighed down our hearts might be under the burden of sin, an echo of Eden remains within them.

John Paul pointed out that the awareness of our sinfulness is a necessary point of departure in historical man, and a condition for aspiring to virtue, purity of heart, and perfection.[44] A general sense of our shortcomings will not suffice. As John Paul noted, Christ "shows how deep down it is necessary to go, how the innermost recesses of the human heart must be thoroughly revealed, so that this heart might become a place in which the law is 'fulfilled.'"[45]

By fulfilled, the Pope did not mean obeyed flawlessly for the sake of conforming to external religious rules. Rather, love is the fulfillment of the law. When one rediscovers the spousal meaning of the body, one can express this through the "interior freedom of the gift."[46]

If the deepest motives of our heart are ruled by the lack of love, which is sin, we are not free to love or to make a gift of ourselves. Moral laws will seem to be nothing more than external constraints that limit our freedom. But when we become aware that the internal constraints of sin are what limit our freedom to love, we will desire to battle against them and experience true liberation. Although this will require us to be demanding toward our heart and our body, true love is not afraid of sacrifice.[47]

## The Problem of Lust

Being free to love sounds appealing, but one major obstacle that stands in the way is lust. Unfortunately, many people equate sexual desire with lust. They assume that if Jesus said that lust is evil, then sexual attraction, pleasure, and passion must be unholy as well. Not only does this keep countless people from pursuing purity, it also becomes a source of great discouragement to those who do pursue it. After all, if sexual desire *is* lust, and the sexual urge can't be extinguished, then purity is not only unhealthy but impossible! Thankfully, purity isn't about dousing sexual desire, but setting it ablaze with love.

If we understand the meaning of lust, it becomes clear why it is the enemy of the most passionate form of love. *Lust is a reduction of a person to his or her sexual value.* As Michael Waldstein explained, it is "when a man or a woman fails to see this full attractiveness of the other person and reduces it to the attractiveness of sexual pleasure alone."[48] This causes individuals—and entire cultures—to measure the worth of people based upon the level of passion they arouse. They become valuable and useful to the degree they are pleasurable. Christopher West rightly noted, "Authentic sexual attraction is always an attraction to the beauty of the other *as a person*, not merely as an object of selfish consumption. This is the enormous value of the virtue of chastity."[49]

Contrary to popular belief, lust does not intensify attractions. It dulls them. Volkmar Sigusch, a German sexologist whose thinking was instrumental in the sexual revolution, observed, "A key feature of sexual revolution is the large-scale publication and commercialization of details that were once secret. Sexuality has been trivialized. The interesting thing about this is that exaggerated portrayals apparently destroy desire more effectively than any repression."[50]

One reason why this happens is because lust doesn't only devalue the person, it diminishes the value of the body and the meaning of attraction. Lust blinds one from seeing the spousal meaning of the body. John Paul used stern language to describe its effects, saying that lust "tramples on the ruins of the spousal meaning of the body and . . . aims directly toward one and only one end as its precise object: *to satisfy only the body's sexual urge.*"[51] This is a deception of the human heart to our calling as men and women.[52] The other person ceases to be a subject of eternal attraction and becomes nothing more than an object of enjoyment.[53]

In the Pope's eyes, lust isn't only a betrayal of love, but a betrayal of what it means to be human. Although many assume that lust is natural, it is more accurate to say that nothing could be more unnatural. If we are made in the image and likeness of love, lust isn't who we are. This is why a person could feast upon lust for decades, only to have an inescapable sense that he or she is starving.

However, as we acquire the virtue of purity, John Paul explained that "we come to an ever greater awareness of the gratuitous beauty of the human body, of masculinity and femininity. This gratuitous beauty becomes a light for our actions."[54] The goal of purity is not to be prudish or puritanical, but to see the mystery of God in and through the body!

**Eros and Agape**
Passion and purity are not rivals. In fact, they require each other to thrive. Many understand how passion can enrich love, but few realize how purity intensifies passion. Even fewer realize how essential passion is for developing purity. One reason why so many people assume that they are irreconcilable is because of a

misunderstanding of the Greek words *agape* and *eros*. These terms are often reduced to mean "God's unconditional love" versus "passionate, erotic love." This oversimplification is misleading.

Michael Waldstein explained, "Following John Paul II, one should avoid an excessive distinction between eros and agape, between sexual fulfillment and the disinterested gift of self in the love between man and woman. It would not be agape, but a slap in the face of one's spouse to say, 'I give myself to you only for your own good. I am not interested in any pleasure you might give me.'"[55] Sacrifice and sensuality are both expressions of spousal love.

John Paul pointed out that for Plato, eros "represents the inner power that draws man toward all that is good, true, and beautiful."[56] Therefore, eros is not the problem. Lust is. Lust cheapens eros and diminishes it. In the relationship between men and women, true eros draws one to the value of the other in the fullness of his or her masculinity and femininity as a person, not just to the sexual value of the body. This balanced idea of eros leaves room for ethos (the innermost values of the person). John Paul explained, "In the erotic sphere, 'eros' and 'ethos' do not diverge, are not opposed to each other, but *are called to meet in the human heart and to bear fruit in this meeting*."[57] Not only is it possible to unite what is erotic to what is ethical, it is necessary. Within marriage, ethos and eros meet.[58]

Although people tend to view ethics as prohibitions and commandments, it is important to unveil the deeper values that these norms protect and assure.[59] The Pope explained:

It is necessary continually to rediscover the spousal meaning of the body and the true dignity of the gift in what is "erotic." This is the task of the human spirit, and it is by its nature an ethical task. If one does not assume this task, the very attraction of the senses and the passion of the body can stop at mere concupiscence, deprived of all ethical value, and man, male and female, does not experience that fullness of "eros," which implies the upward impulse of the human spirit toward what is true, good, and beautiful, so that what is "erotic" also becomes true, good, and beautiful.[60]

Jesus did not come merely to redeem the souls of the lost, but to reclaim our humanity—body and soul—with all that makes us human, including our sexual desires. Therefore, the transformation of eros is an integral part of Christian life.[61] Again, this is not about dampening desire. Rather, John Paul explained that putting these principles into practice makes expressions of affection "spiritually more intense and thus *enriches* them."[62]

Therefore, not only are eros and agape not rivals, they rely upon each other to reach their perfection. In the words of John Paul, "Agape brings eros to fulfillment while purifying it."[63] Or, as one Orthodox theologian explained, "Without agape, eros remains stunted, partial—finally it collapses and isn't even eros; the fire goes out and all that remains is the original concern with the self. Such eros has never risen above self-love."[64] Because it is rooted in self-love, unchastity is "the total defeat of eros."[65] It is a weak and incomplete form of desire. On the other hand, "Chastity is eros in its holy form."[66]

The *Catechism* echoes this, saying that purity "lets us perceive the human body—ours and our neighbor's—as a . . . manifestation of divine beauty."[67] We might have an intellectual idea of a person's dignity, but if we are driven by lust, we don't deeply feel and experience this reality. In the beginning, eros was given to be the power to love as God loves. It was a foretaste and invitation to the ultimate fulfillment of eros in the eternal communion with God, and he wants to restore its original purpose.

These theological insights sound beautiful, but they might seem so heavenly that we may wonder how they relate to our earthly lives. How is such passionate purity possible when our hearts and minds are so often muddled by sin? Is it really possible to see the human body as a "manifestation of divine beauty"?

## Love Swallows Up Shame
While many people assume that modesty is synonymous with ample clothing (picture an ankle-length,

shapeless plaid jumper), John Paul's vision is deeper. He declared, "Purity is the glory of the human body before God. It is the glory of God in the human body, through which masculinity and femininity are manifested."[68]

To some, this definition of purity may be a Copernican shift from all that they have learned about the body. It isn't bad or dirty. If it were, then there would be no pure way to view it. Spouses would be incapable of modesty and purity, as would artists, doctors, and so on. But how does one protect the meaning of the body from concupiscence?

In *Love and Responsibility*, he explained:

> Man, alas, is not such a perfect being that the sight of the body of another person, especially a person of the other sex, can arouse in him merely a disinterested liking which develops into an innocent affection. In practice, it also arouses concupiscence, or a wish to enjoy concentrated on sexual values with no regard for the value of the person.[69]

The Pope understood the reality of temptation. He knew that effort is required on behalf of each person to order his or her desires according to the demands of authentic love. But in time and with the aid of grace, this task begins to feel more natural. One's relationships with others—including those of the opposite sex—are characterized by greater simplicity and freedom.[70] He added:

We can find God in everything, we can commune with him in and through all things. Created things cease to be a danger for us as once they were, particularly while we were still at the purgative stage of our journey. Creation, and other people in particular, not only regain their true light, given to them by God the Creator, but, so to speak, they lead us to God himself.[71]

While encouraging all people to strive toward this purification, John Paul received widespread criticism after one of his Theology of the Body audiences in which he said that husbands should not lust after their wives.[72] In saying this, he was not scolding men for being sexually attracted to their wives. He was reminding them not to view their spouses as objects to be used for their gratification.

More precisely, he was encouraging them to bless their brides with the peaceful reassurance that only comes from pure desire. As mentioned earlier, in the beginning Eve experienced "all the peace of the interior gaze." Something similar happens within a holy marriage. In the presence of genuine love, shame loses its reason for existence. As he explains in *Love and Responsibility*, shame is "swallowed up by love, dissolved into it so that the man and the woman are no longer ashamed to be sharing their experience of sexual values."[73] The way that husbands and wives express affection ought to protect this peace.[74]

## Masters of Suspicion

John Paul's vision of human love is a hopeful one because it contradicts the widespread notion—even within Christianity—that lust is the only way to view the human body. If we give in to this pessimism, not only do we forfeit the hope of love, we become, according to the Pope, "masters of suspicion."[75]

Against this mindset, John Paul proclaimed:

> We cannot stop at the mere accusation of the human heart on the basis of the desire and concupiscence of the flesh. *Man cannot stop at casting the heart into a state of* continual and irreversible *suspicion.* . . . Redemption is a truth, a reality, in the name of which man must feel himself called, and "called with effectiveness."[76]

This point has major implications for living out the Theology of the Body. John Paul insisted, "The meaning of life is the antithesis of the [interpretation] 'of suspicion.'"[77] If it is impossible to look upon the human body rightly, then its spousal meaning remains veiled. Our call to love like God becomes suffocated under a never-ending predisposition to use. Although it is necessary to acknowledge the presence of concupiscence, we can't define man by concupiscence alone.[78] There is a greater potential in the human heart than our weakened wills and disordered appetites. The Pope explained:

It is important that precisely in his "heart" he does not feel himself irrevocably accused and given up to the concupiscence of the flesh, but that in the same heart he feels himself called with energy. Called precisely to this supreme value, which is love. Called as a person in the truth of his humanity, and thus also in the truth of his masculinity and femininity, in the truth of his body. Called in that truth which has been his inheritance "of the beginning," the inheritance of his heart, which is deeper than the sinfulness inherited, deeper than the threefold concupiscence. Christ's words, set in the whole reality of creation and redemption, reactivate that deepest inheritance and give it real power in human life.[79]

John Paul asked:

What are the "concrete possibilities of man"? And of *which* man are we speaking? Of man *dominated* by lust or of man *redeemed by Christ?* This is what is at stake: the *reality* of Christ's redemption. *Christ has redeemed us!* This means that he has given us the possibility of realizing *the entire* truth of our being; he has set our freedom free from the *domination* of concupiscence.[80]

Ponder these words. The words of Jesus have the power to reactivate the deepest inheritance of the human heart and give it power!

**Negative and Positive Purity**

How can these words of the Pope be reconciled with the many admonitions in Scripture to look away from occasions of sin? For example, Sirach 9:8 warns, "Turn away your eyes from a shapely woman, and do not look intently at beauty belonging to another; many have been misled by a woman's beauty, and by it passion is kindled like a fire." These words do not lose their validity, because they remain a first step toward purity. John Paul would consider them a form of "negative purity."

Unfortunately, many remain there, not realizing that one should look *away* from temptations in order to look *into* our own hearts and *up* to God, to learn how to see the other as a person. As one priest noted, "Purity of heart is not found primarily in what we turn away from, but in Whom we turn toward."[81] Looking away isn't the ultimate goal. Learning how to see is the goal. This is why Jesus called the pure in heart "blessed." Not only will they see God in the next life, they see him in this life throughout creation, revealed especially in their bodies and the bodies of others. Their purity exists not despite the body, but in and through it.[82]

This is what the Pope considered "positive" purity.[83] John Paul explained that in Christ's Sermon on the Mount, the Old Testament law prohibiting adultery "becomes an invitation to a pure way of looking at others, capable of respecting the spousal meaning of the body."[84] We should not be motivated to love merely by our intellect or willpower, but also by our heart.

43

John Paul proposed that "this truth must be known in an interior way; it must in some way be 'felt with the heart,' so that the reciprocal relations between man and woman—and even mere looks—may regain that authentically spousal content of their meanings."[85]

The Holy Father noted that the act of looking at another person is really an interior act expressed by looking.[86] It is not an insignificant glance. This is why Saint Augustine warned, "Do not say that you have a chaste mind if you have unchaste eyes, because an unchaste eye is the messenger of an unchaste heart."[87] Christopher West added that men will often wait until a woman is not looking in order to look lustfully at her.[88] One solution to this (for both men and women) is only to look upon another's body as if he or she were looking back into your eyes.

Although lust is not a problem only for males, the Pope extended a particular challenge in this area to the men. He reminded them: "The woman has 'from the beginning' been entrusted to his eyes, . . . to his 'heart,'" and he must ensure that the exchange of the gift "creates an authentic communion of persons."[89] He has been charged with the responsibility of being *"the guardian of the reciprocity of the gift."*[90] "Although maintaining the balance of the gift seems to be something entrusted to both, the man has a special responsibility, as if it depended more on him whether the balance is kept or violated or even—if it has already been violated—reestablished."[91] He added that the dignity and balance of human life "depend at every moment of history and in every place of geographic longitude and latitude on 'who' she shall be for him and he for her."[92]

Men should not feel as if the Pope was singling them out to judge them. His words are a noble exhortation to examine one's deepest motives. He's challenging men to look within themselves and answer one question: "Who has she become for me?"[93] Men and women do not need to live in shame of their own passions. What they need is the humility to bring those desires to Christ.

God does not want his sons and daughters to live under the yoke of scrupulosity. Fr. Alexander Men, a Russian Orthodox priest and biblical scholar, wrote about a group of ancient Pharisees who wanted so ardently to avoid sin that they would not lift their eyes. They walked with their heads bowed, lest they see a woman and lust after her. Eventually, others began calling them "*Khitsay*," which means: "Don't hit your head."[94] Although this may have been a primitive form of negative purity, it's not the message of Christ.

Again, the problem is not the body. The problem is how it's portrayed and how we view it. It isn't supposed to be an occasion of sin, but a revelation of our call to love. It wasn't created to tempt us toward hell, but to remind us of the beauty of heaven. When sunlight enters a diamond, countless miniature reflections of the jewel burst forth, bathed in color. Similarly, the beauty of the human body is a faint reflection of the infinite beauty of its source: the Holy Trinity. God reveals himself to mankind through each experience of beauty. The question is whether or not we have the eyes to see beyond the reflection . . . to the source of its glory.

## Nudity and Art

Those who have had the blessing of visiting Saint Peter's Basilica in the Vatican may recall the beams of sunlight streaming across its vast interior, the magnificence of Michelangelo's Pietà, or the seven-story tall baldacchino that looms over the high altar. What few notice, however, is the sculpture of the virtue of virginity—depicted as a bare-breasted woman—that lounges amidst dozens of others, looking down upon the congregation.

Imagine when the seventeenth-century sculpture was created and hoisted above the arches in the main nave of the church. Didn't anyone question the prudence of depicting purity with an icon so . . . immodest? Apparently not. They weren't immersed in a pornified culture, and therefore didn't equate nudity with immodesty.

In order for an artistic rendering of the human body to serve its purpose, both the artist and the viewer must safeguard the value of the person depicted. Therefore, when discussing nudity and art, John Paul spoke of the ethos of the image and the ethos of viewing.[95] When artists create, they are showing their "inner world of values."[96] Depending upon how they portray the body, its value can be deepened and formed, or deformed and destroyed.[97] Therefore, the artist has a responsibility to know and reveal the whole truth about man. Sacred nude art doesn't aim to push the viewer toward lust, but toward learning the spousal meaning of the body. Because the body is a revelation of God's plan for love, it is very good and therefore should not be portrayed as an object of one's gratification. To determine the goodness of art, one could ask, "In this image, is the body revealing the person or distracting the viewer from seeing his or her value?"

Pornography is a prime example of imagery that deforms the value of the person. Why is nude sacred art considered modest while pornography is not? A clear reason is offered in *Love and Responsibility*: "Immodesty is present only when nakedness plays a negative role with regard to the value of the person, when its aim is to arouse concupiscence, as a result of which the person is put in the position of an object of enjoyment."[98] Therefore, pornography is immoral not because it is addictive or often induces sexual dysfunction. It's wrong because it is utilitarian. People were not created to be used.

By pointing this out, John Paul was not being puritanical; he was acknowledging the value of the body. Despite their claims, pornographers do not have a greater appreciation of the body than the Pope. Modesty requires awe and wonder at the dignity of the body, but such reverence is absent in pornography, where the value of the person is sacrificed on the altar of lust. When this happens, addiction takes the place of awe, and restless curiosity followed by inevitable boredom becomes a sad substitute for wonder.

The Pope never argued that pornography is bad because the body is bad. It's wrong because the body is so good. To him, it's not immoral because it shows too much of the person, but because it shows too little. It displaces the body—and therefore the person—out of its proper context (love), much like extracting a fish out of the ocean. Instead of revealing the whole person, it exposes the body. This is why pornography is considered "obscene." This term comes from the Latin word *obscaena*, which means "that which should not be seen by spectators."[99]

Those who portray the human body aren't the only ones responsible for the way it is viewed. The ones who look upon it are also presented with a task. An artist could create an image with the purest of motives, and yet have his or her masterpiece become an object of lust for those whose hearts are bent toward that vice.

It is natural to desire to see the beauty of the human body. This desire isn't evil. Each person has a God-given desire to behold what is beautiful. But John Paul reminded his listeners that one cannot ignore the fact that historical man is in a state of concupiscence.[100] Everyone is tempted to sin. However, shame can be overcome without overstepping it. But the Pope noted that this involves "difficulty and inner resistance."[101]

For those whom John Paul described as "masters of suspicion," the solution to the problems of shame and lust isn't the path of "difficulty and inner resistance," but the removal of the challenge itself. This is why, when Michelangelo painted nudes throughout the Sistine Chapel, some within the Church demanded that the bodies be covered up. After Michelangelo's death, many were painted over with loincloths and were concealed for centuries, until John Paul commissioned a team of restoration artists to remove many of the loincloths and uncover Michelangelo's original design. Those who concealed the bodies likely prided themselves on their purity. However, by covering the sacred art, they were revealing their inability to see the spousal meaning of the body, and thus, their own impurity.

## Pure Intimacy

The task of safeguarding the goodness of the body in its nakedness extends beyond art. It must also be protected within marriage. As mentioned above, the global media mocked and criticized John Paul when he explained that Christ's prohibition against lust includes lust for one's own spouse. In his words, "Adultery 'in the heart' is not committed only because the man 'looks' in this way at a woman who is not his wife, but *precisely because he looks in this way at a woman. Even* if he were to look in this way at the woman who is his wife, he would commit the same adultery 'in the heart.'"[102] Christ speaks of "a woman," not just a woman who is the wife of another.[103]

The criticism leveled against the Pope was based on one glaring oversight on the part of the media: sexual attraction is not equivalent to lust. The Pope wasn't condemning passion. He was reminding the Church that lust remains a threat to love even within marriage because it is *a reduction of a person to his or her sexual value.* It is a reduction that blocks intimacy. In the words of John Paul, it reduces "the whole personal richness of femininity [and masculinity] to this one value."[104]

Some might ask, "But how can a person be guilty of adultery without actually committing it?"[105] John Paul answered that lust reduces the purpose of the woman's existence "for" the man "to the mere satisfaction of the body's sexual 'urge.'"[106] When a look is detached from the spousal and procreative meanings of the body, it ceases to be a look of genuine love.[107] It is adultery in the heart. He added that God "assigns the dignity of every woman as a task to every man . . . [and] he assigns also the dignity of every man to every woman."[108] Therefore, the obligation to uphold the dignity of one's spouse should be especially important.

Although sensuality isn't evil, it is blind to the value of the person.[109] It is a spontaneous and natural reaction that must be directed by each person by love, so that the sexual reactions are raised to the personal level.[110] Therefore, purity isn't the lack of something. It is an *ability,* centered on the dignity of the body, to view the entire person.[111] It is lust that limits one's vision to the sexual values of the other. As a result, lust robs sex of its depth.

Some have defined intimacy as "into-me-see," but how is such closeness possible when one cannot see beyond the skin? Purity is not about seeing less of the body, but about seeing more of the person. This, John Paul said, "creates precisely the fullness of the intimacy of persons."[112] When such purity of heart is present, the desire to do what is best for the other takes precedence over the urge to pursue mere enjoyment. While lust leads individuals to focus on their own desires alone, true ecstasy takes us out of ourselves. No wonder John Paul declared that "purity is a requirement of love" that brings about a deeper experience of it.[113]

It is not abstinence that makes one pure. Jesus never said, "Blessed are the abstinent." While abstinence can be one form of expressing purity, a person does not become less pure by entering into marriage and experiencing God's gift of sexual intimacy. But one must realize that this is holy ground. Not only is it an open invitation to the Holy Spirit, who is the Lord and Giver of Life, it is a renewal of one's wedding vows in the flesh.

### True Spontaneity

All this religious talk about sexual intimacy might lead some to ask, "Doesn't purity ruin spontaneity?" This is a fair question and John Paul spent a considerable amount of time offering a thoughtful reply to it.

In *Love and Responsibility*, he notes that chastity is often seen as the enemy of love because sensual and emotional reactions are often confused with love.[114]

The sexual urge is part of human nature, and therefore is not the problem. The problem is when concupiscence distorts this urge in such a way that sexual pleasure becomes more valuable than the person. Chastity corrects this distortion, because it orders one's sexual desires according to the demands of love.

Chastity is not the cause of sexual tension, but the solution to it.[115] If indulgence removed sexual tension, one's appetite for pleasure would not return so quickly or become more demanding over time. Instead of viewing chastity as an obstacle to obtaining gratification, it should be viewed as a litmus test of love. Whereas love is not afraid to suffer to do the good, lust reveals selfishness and cowardice.

John Paul explained that at first, one experiences self-control as an ability to resist temptation. It may feel artificial, forced, and restrictive. But in time, it matures into the capacity to perceive, love, and realize the meaning of the body, which is unknown to lust.[116] Through it, men and women gradually discover their dignity and "the freedom of the gift."[117] The law against lust no longer feels like a burden to the degree that Christ has redeemed one's heart. Rather than seeing purity as a boring restriction, it becomes the key to true spontaneity.

Michael Waldstein points out that "spontaneous" does not mean unplanned and impulsive, but comes from the Latin *spons,* which can mean "free will." It means the person's free will is the source of the action, rather than carnal instinct or addiction.[118] John Paul added, "At the price of mastery over these impulses, man reaches that *deeper and more mature spontaneity* with which his 'heart,' by mastering the instincts, rediscovers the spiritual beauty of the sign constituted by the human body in its masculinity and femininity."[119] One of the many fruits of self-mastery is that men and women gain this deepened sense of the dignity of the other in their heart.[120] They realize that the human body possesses a beauty that goes beyond the physical level.[121]

Spontaneity is a good thing. In fact, John Paul insisted that each person is "*called to full and mature spontaneity* in relationships that are born from the perennial attraction of masculinity and femininity. Such spontaneity is itself the gradual fruit of the discernment of the impulses of one's own heart."[122] He adds that one should not be afraid to discern the movements of one's heart. Instead, one should be "the authentic master of his own innermost impulses, like a watchman who watches over a hidden spring."[123] If one perseveres in doing this, the "human heart comes to share, so to speak, in another spontaneity of which the 'carnal man' knows nothing or very little."[124]

When lust reigns in the heart, one might feel liberated from external constraints, but a closer look reveals many internal constraints that rob the person of freedom. For example, if someone lacks self-control, is that person free to make a gift of himself or herself? The Pope remarked, "The satisfaction of the passions is one thing, but the joy that man finds in mastering himself more fully is another thing, since in this way, he can make a gift of himself to another."[125]

While some are constrained by sin, others are enslaved by fear. One such example is those who are afraid that they will lose themselves if they make a serious commitment to their vocations. But man is not enslaved by commitment, only by the fear of it. This anxiety keeps many from finding themselves by making a gift of themselves. Whether it is sin or fear that binds a person, the Word of God declares: "For freedom Christ has set us free" (Gal. 5:1). Such freedom is the key to spontaneity.

## Life According to the Spirit

In this life, purity is never acquired once and for all.[126] It requires a gradual and continual shaping of the heart's desires and movements. Those who attempt to practice chastity soon learn that purity doesn't begin to grow until a person realizes that one cannot rely upon human efforts alone. It is not primarily man's work. It is a gift from God.[127] As Saint John Vianney noted, "Temptation is necessary to make us realize that we are nothing in ourselves."[128]

As a young man, Saint Augustine lived a promiscuous life, but later experienced a renewal of purity following his conversion. Looking back upon the struggle to change his ways, he recalled, "I thought that continence arose from one's own powers, which I did not recognize in myself. I was foolish enough not to know . . . that no one can be continent unless you [Lord] grant it. For you would surely have granted it if my inner groaning had reached your ears and I with firm faith had cast my cares on you."[129]

John Paul likewise taught that in order to have purity of heart, one must become open to life according to the Spirit.[130] Purity is a fruit of the Holy Spirit, and in John Paul's words, this "underlines *God's action* in human beings."[131] Each person is called to become— like the Virgin Mary—actively receptive to the gift of the Holy Spirit in order to be fruitful with Christ.

When one begins to live life according to the Spirit, a transformation can begin that extends much deeper than one's external behavior. John Paul not only declared that man can experience a "real and deep victory" over lust, but that this victory can and should be realized in the human heart![132] He explained, "In mature purity, man enjoys the fruits of victory over concupiscence."[133] If you recall, original sin left man with a darkened intellect, a weakened will, and disordered appetites. Consider how life in the Spirit works to heal these wounds of sin.

Sin darkens the intellect and lust blinds one to the meaning of the body. Life according to the Spirit opens one's eyes to it.[134] The Pope remarked that as our awareness of this matures, "it opens the way toward an ever more perfect discovery of the dignity of the human body."[135]

Sin also weakens the will and disorders one's appetites. But life according to the Spirit helps one to regain the interior freedom of the gift. With the mature development of a virtue, choosing the good happens with greater ease and joy because one's desires are ordered rightly. All too often, people think about morality as simply the following of an ethic (an external rule) without a change of ethos (one's inner values).[136] As a result, these individuals give up too easily. If they remain cut off from being able to love as God loves, they miss the meaning of life.

Redemption is not about overpowering the desires of our hearts, but about healing and transforming our desires so that we yearn for what is truly good. Bending our wills to follow the letter of the law is not the point of the gospel. We ought to be moved to choose the good not simply through a cold and gritty decision driven by our intellect or our will, but also by our heart.[137] Gradually, our subjective desires can come into conformity with the objective meaning of the body. This isn't about ethical truth only, but about the truth of what it means to be human.[138]

### Piety

Imagine if there was a gift that could restore to the body—especially in the relationship between men and women—"all *its simplicity, its lucid clarity,* and also *its interior joy.*"[139] Who would not want to receive this? This gift does exist, and according to John Paul, it is the gift of piety. Although most people associate this term with those who have a hyperreligious devotional life and are perhaps a bit prudish, this is not what John Paul had in mind.

Saint Paul declared that the will of God is that each Christian knows "how to keep his own body with holiness and reverence."[140] More than abstinence or self-restraint, piety is a deep reverence for all things sacred, including the body. If sin dulls our understanding of the meaning of the body and the value of sexuality, piety heightens our sensitivity to the dignity that the body possesses.[141] It is the crowning of chastity, and according to John Paul, "turns out to be the most essential power for keeping the body 'with holiness.'"[142] It is the Holy Spirit who empowers each person to view his or her body—and the bodies of others—with such reverence.

Saint Paul also explained why Christians should have such reverence for their bodies when he asked, "Do you not know your body is a temple?"[143] The Holy Spirit dwells in man and in his body as in a temple, and this Gift is what makes every human being holy.[144] Many Christians have heard so often that their body is a temple of the Holy Spirit that the phrase has become almost meaningless. Yet if one pauses to consider the reality of his or her body being a dwelling place of the Blessed Trinity, a newfound appreciation of the body can develop. This deep appreciation of the value of the body and sexuality is the only foundation upon which true purity can be built.

Through the gift of piety, one realizes that lustful indulgence or prudish repression aren't the only two options when temptations arise. One can recognize the goodness of the body, and instead of merely restraining one's urges, raise them toward heaven. One begins to practice the habit of quickly affirming the value of the person when concupiscence inclines us to value only the body. This may begin out of a desire to avoid offending God, but with time it blooms into a desire to glorify God in one's body. Because of sin, this habit requires effort and does not come naturally. However, John Paul declared, "Yet, this meaning was to *remain as a task given to man . . .* inscribed in the depth of the human heart as a distant echo, as it were, of original innocence."[145]

3

# CHRIST APPEALS TO THE RESURRECTION

**Eschatological Man**

In the third and final key word of Christ, John Paul reflected upon Jesus' dialogue with the Sadducees, when the religious leaders presented the following dilemma to him in an effort to disprove the resurrection of the body:

> There were seven brothers; the first married and, when he died, left no children; and the second married her and died, leaving no children; and the third likewise; none of the seven left children. Last of all the woman herself died. In the resurrection, when they will rise, whose wife will she be? For the seven had married her. (Mark 12:20–23)

Jesus replied:

> Is not this the reason you are wrong, that you know neither the Scriptures nor the power of God? For when they rise from the dead, they take neither wife nor husband, but are like angels in heaven. (Mark 12:24–25)

59

Two aspects of Christ's reply often raise questions for the reader. He asserts the absence of human marriage in heaven and affirms we will be "like angels." By comparing our heavenly state to that of the angels, he is not implying that we will live without bodies, but that we will be unmarried.[1]

Many people assume that upon death they will be released from the bondage of their corruptible bodies to live eternally as pure spirits. While Christianity affirms the immortality of the soul, it also proclaims the resurrection of the *body*. Our future destiny is a bodily reality, and it is an error to think of our bodies as disposable cages that house our immortal souls. In fact, we don't understand our own humanity without understanding this. It's less than human to eternally exist as a disincarnated spirit or as a body stripped of its soul. This is why Peter Kreeft remarked, "That is why we are terrified of ghosts and corpses, though both are harmless: they are the obscenely separated aspects of what belongs together as one."[2]

What will our glorified bodies be? John Paul explained that we will have a "spiritualized body." Such a term tends to confuse the modern mind, as if he said our bodies will be "invisibly visible." But this error comes from our mistaken notion of human nature. It's not natural for man to experience a lack of harmony between our souls and our bodies, even though that is our unhappy inheritance due to original sin. In the beginning, it was not so. And likewise in the end, it will not be so.

What he means by a spiritualized body is that the power of the spirit will fully permeate the body.[3] We will no longer experience opposition between the body and soul. Rather, we will live in an integrated way, because the body and soul will be perfectly united.[4] This is not a victory of the spirit over the body, but the full realization of what it means to be human.[5]

## Heavenly Marriage

Another difficulty that arises in Christ's reply is that human marriage will cease to exist in the next life. While some might assume that the absence of marriage in heaven diminishes its importance, the opposite is true. From the beginning, marriage has been a sign of God's love for man and his plan of salvation for us. It points us to the wedding feast described in the book of Revelation.

Our bodies reveal that we are made for communion through a sincere gift of ourselves. But earthly relationships cannot ultimately fulfill our deepest yearnings. Human love, as intoxicating as it may be, is only a shadow and a sign of the reality of what we have been created for—ecstatic, blissful, loving union with the Blessed Trinity in heaven. If this is God's purpose for the one-flesh union between man and woman on earth, then one could argue that the absence of marital intimacy in heaven reveals its glory! With what awe and reverence should men and women treat the gift of sexuality if it has been given to us for such a majestic purpose!

Because the human body reveals that man is created for communion, heaven will be our ultimate fulfillment. It is the perfect realization of the spousal meaning of the body. As the Holy Father explained, "The absolute and eternal spousal meaning of the glorified body will be revealed in union with God himself, by seeing him 'face to face.'"[6] Only in heaven will we be capable of fully giving ourselves to God without reserve, with no taint of sin. Likewise, only in heaven will we be capable of fully receiving God's total gift of himself to us.[7]

In the life to come, God will not merely be revealed to us, as if heaven were nothing more than a vast sea of people admiring his glory. John Paul explained that the grace of God will not only be revealed "in all its penetrating depth, but will also be experienced in its beatifying reality."[8] Through this, we will experience "full participation in God's inner life, that is, in trinitarian Reality itself."[9]

In a remarkable statement, John Paul declared that God will communicate himself "*in his very divinity,* not only to the soul, but *to the whole of man's psychosomatic subjectivity.*"[10] This theologically dense statement means that God's grace won't merely sanctify our souls, but will permeate our bodies as well! We will participate in the inner life of God himself, and in this state, "penetration and permeation of what is essentially human by what is essentially divine, will then reach its peak, so that the life of the human spirit will reach a fullness that was absolutely inaccessible to it before."[11] As Catholics, this should not shock us, because we pray in every Mass that we might "come to share in the divinity of Christ, who humbled himself to share in our humanity."

This unspeakable union with the Trinity will not absorb us or diminish our individuality. Rather, our intimate union with God will make us fully human.[12] For this reason, sainthood should be understood as the full bloom of the human person—both body and soul. In him, we rediscover ourselves, and what it means to be created for communion. If love yearns for total union, heaven will satisfy the human heart like nothing on earth ever could.

After explaining the eternal plan of God for our bodies and souls in heaven, John Paul turned his attention to how some men and women choose to anticipate this reality on earth.

### Celibacy for the Kingdom
At the beginning of his reflections, John Paul examined the discussion between Jesus and the Pharisees regarding the topic of divorce. He now returned to this same passage to conclude the exchange:

> Because of the hardness of your heart Moses allowed you to divorce your wives, but from the beginning it was not so. Therefore I say to you, Whoever divorces his wife, except in the case of

[unlawful marriage], and marries another commits adultery. (Matt. 19:8–9)

Upon hearing this, his disciples make an astonishing reply: "If this is the condition of man in relation to woman, it is not advantageous to marry" (Matt. 19:10). Put plainly: "If you can't get divorced, then it's better not to get married!"

Instead of addressing their hearts—which seem harder than the Pharisees—or arguing about whether or not marriage is "advantageous," Jesus replies:

Not all can understand it, *but only those to whom it has been granted.* For there are eunuchs who were born this way from their mother's womb; there are some who were made eunuchs by men, and there are others who *made themselves eunuchs for the kingdom of heaven.* Let anyone understand this who can." (Matt. 19:11–12)

Eunuchs were men incapable of having intercourse because of a physical defect caused by nature or by an act such as castration. In ancient cultures, eunuchs would often be employed as guards and attendants for the queen because they had no choice but to be abstinent. However, Jesus mentions a third kind of eunuch, who has *chosen* to forgo marriage "for the kingdom of heaven." This would have been a bewildering concept for most Jews at the time, because celibacy was not valued.

Furthermore, why would Jesus lead into his invitation to celibacy by drawing such unpleasant comparisons?

John Paul explained:

*Jesus in some way touches upon all of these backgrounds,* as if he wanted to say, I know that what I am going to tell you now will raise great difficulties in your consciousness, in your way of understanding the meaning of the body; I shall speak to you, in fact, about continence, and this will undoubtedly be associated in you with a state of physical deficiency, inborn or acquired by human cause. I want to tell you, by contrast, that continence can also be voluntary and chosen by man "for the kingdom of heaven."[13]

Jesus is introducing his disciples to a radical new way of living as a gift for others. While some might think of celibacy as unnatural, Jesus clarifies that it can be *supernatural* when freely chosen for the kingdom.

But why would anyone willingly choose to be celibate? Didn't God say it wasn't good for man to be alone? Indeed, it isn't good for man to be alone, but only God can fulfill the ache of solitude created by our aloneness. Even if a person has a spouse, he or she is still alone before God.

Those who forgo marriage to enter the priesthood or religious life are not doing so because they have no desire to make a gift of themselves to another. In fact, love alone explains the motive and means of both the married and the celibate vocations. Both vocations involve a radical decision to give one's self away to another to live in communion. Both are the result of a person freely responding to the love of another. And both are made possible by the freedom of the gift, obtained through self-mastery. It's not as though celibacy requires self-mastery while marriage offers an outlet for lust. Rather, both vocations require self-control so that one may make a gift of one's self. All are called to master their desires so that they can be free to love. Therefore, both vocations have a spousal nature.

Jesus exemplifies this, showing how virginity can be an expression of the spousal meaning of the body. His love for his bride, the Church, echoes through history at every Mass: "This is my body, given up for you." This total self-giving is also lived out in the men and women who consecrate their lives to the service of the Church. As one woman exclaimed to a group of religious sisters, "You must give over your life as you would toss a flower."[14]

Because of the spousal meaning of the body, in one way or another every man is called to fatherhood and every woman to motherhood. This calling is stamped into every body. John Paul explained that the man's body has a paternal meaning, while *the mystery of femininity manifests and reveals itself in its full depth through motherhood.*[15]

But how can this be fulfilled when one chooses to forgo marriage? Celibacy for the sake of the kingdom is an act of spousal love, and therefore it is an act of fruitful love: It is ordered toward fatherhood and motherhood.[16] When men and women choose a celibate vocation, they are not renouncing their God-given desire to become mothers and fathers. Rather, they are fulfilling this calling in a different manner.

The physical fruitfulness of husbands and wives is a sign of the spiritual fruitfulness of those who choose celibacy for the sake of the kingdom. When a woman enters religious life, she expresses her gift of self in a uniquely feminine way. As seen in the Blessed Virgin Mary, who is the model of fruitful virginity, virginity blooms in spiritual motherhood. Likewise, a man who enters the priesthood does not leave his masculinity behind when he joins the seminary. Rather, he is being called to lay down his life for his bride, the Church, as Saint Paul challenged all husbands to do (Eph. 5). His contribution to the Church is uniquely masculine and therefore paternal. Thus, all priests are called "Father."

Celibacy for the sake of the kingdom has been, and will always be, a sign of contradiction. But in no way is it a rejection of one's sexuality as male and female. Nor is it a devaluation of marriage. In fact, the renunciation of marriage is an affirmation of its worth. For example, no one gives up eating dirt for Lent. Rather, the value of a sacrifice can be determined by what is being offered. In order to be fully aware of what one is choosing, one must be fully aware of what one is renouncing.[17]

But celibacy isn't merely a sacrifice that certain people offer to God. It is also a gift that God offers to them.[18] When addressing the Sadducees, Jesus explained, "When they rise from the dead, they will take neither wife nor husband" (Mark 12:25). In saying this, he shows that there is a condition of life without marriage, where men and women will live in communion with God and one other. Those who accept the call to celibacy for the sake of the kingdom anticipate in this life what man will experience in the future resurrection.

By forgoing the earthly sign of the ultimate union that we are created for in heaven, celibates offer the world a visible witness that we shouldn't get stuck on the sign. By making a total gift of themselves to God in this life, they become an icon of the life to come. In doing so, they are not encouraging us to reject our sexuality, but are reminding us of the ultimate purpose and meaning of it! Celibacy for the sake of the kingdom is a sign that indicates that the body tends toward glorification. This is why the sacramentality of marriage can only be understood in light of the true meaning of celibacy, and celibacy can only be fully understood in light of marriage.[19] Because both vocations are linked together, any culture that fails to value one will be incapable of valuing the other.

# PART 2

# THE SACRAMENT

4

# THE DIMENSION OF COVENANT AND GRACE

**Analogy of Spousal Love**

Throughout Scripture, the sacred authors use countless analogies to speak of God and his love for mankind. He is the rock, the good shepherd, the sheep gate, and so on. However, these are literary devices. It's not as if God specifically created a gate to be *the* sign of his love, or a rock to reveal the deepest reality about him. But what if God did do this? What if he specifically created one thing to be *the* fundamental sign of who he is and how he loves? He did, and the sign is marriage. It comes from the Father, not from the world.[1]

Some might retort: "The marriages I've seen don't exactly resemble anything from heaven." However, in the beginning, it was not so. In the beginning, the mystery of God became visible through what John Paul called "the primordial sacrament of marriage." But because of original sin, it was "deprived of the supernatural efficaciousness" it had at the beginning.[2] Its ability to reflect and transmit the love of God was diminished.

Like all analogies, there is both similarity and dissimilarity. But of all the possible analogies that explain the love of God, it is the least inadequate one. Therefore, it is the image most commonly used throughout Scripture to explain God's love for humanity. In fact, John Paul called it "the central theme of the whole of revelation."[3]

The Bible begins with a marriage (Adam and Eve) and ends with a marriage (the wedding feast in heaven). Throughout the Old Testament, the prophets spoke of the relationship between God and Israel in marital terms.[4] When Israel abandoned God and turned to idols, this infidelity pierced his heart as Father, Bridegroom, and Lord.[5] However, God forgave this act of spiritual adultery and betrothed Israel to himself.[6]

The New Testament is likewise filled with marital imagery to describe God's plan for salvation: John the Baptist is the friend of the bridegroom, the Church is the bride, Jesus is the groom, and heaven is the wedding feast.[7] God is proposing his love for humanity, and his eternal plan is for us to become one with him in never-ending bliss. Our unity with God in heaven is not like a drop of water that loses its identity when immersed in the ocean. Rather, it is more like two spouses who become one in love, and yet retain their own individuality.

All of creation reveals something of God, and thus John Paul spoke of the "sacrament of creation." However, marriage is its central point.[8] It makes visible the invisible plan of God for man: to participate in Trinitarian life. This is what the body—in its masculinity and femininity—invites us to share in.

According to the *Catechism*, the joys of married life are but "a foretaste of the wedding feast of the Lamb."[9] In saying this, the Church is not sexualizing heaven, as if it's just a more intense experience of sexual union. Rather, our sexuality, when oriented rightly, points us to the source of ultimate fulfillment, which is God.

## Ephesians 5

As shocking as that language may be for some to read, John Paul noted that what was barely outlined and half open in the Old Testament is fully unveiled in Ephesians 5.[10] He considers this chapter of Scripture the crowning of the themes that flow through the Word of God.[11]

In it, Saint Paul begins:

> Wives, be subject to your husbands as you are to the Lord. For the husband is the head of the wife as Christ is the head of the Church, he who is the Savior of his body. And as the Church is subject to Christ, so also wives ought to be subject to their husbands in everything.[12]

This first section of the passage often gives readers the greatest difficulty: The wife ought to be *subject* to her husband? The husband is *savior* of the wife? For many, this sounds like male egoism, patriarchal dominance, and sexist servitude. Genesis 3:16 states that one of the results of original sin is that the woman's desire shall be for her husband, and he shall rule over her.

A chapter earlier, Genesis refers to the woman as the man's "help." Is she some kind of subservient partner to him, and is this really what Saint Paul had in mind?

Genesis 2:18 does speak of the woman as the man's *ezer*, which means "help." However, this is not a derogatory term or a synonym for "maid." In fact, it is a title given repeatedly to God himself.[13] The woman "helps" man be fully human and realize his call to love. He recognizes and finds his humanity with her help.[14]

In terms of Genesis 3:16, Saint Paul is not reiterating the disordered relationship between men and women caused by sin, but is correcting it. John Paul declared that male domination of a woman not only demeans the woman, it also "diminishes the true dignity of the man."[15] Any man who uses his strength to control a woman shows that he is too weak to control himself. He seeks to rule another because doing so is easier than ruling his own pride, lust, anger, selfishness, and so on. This is the brokenness that Paul is seeking to heal.

Even so, how can one reconcile his words about subjection or submission with the dignity women possess? John Paul explained that when this passage is read in context, the wife's submission to the husband signifies above all the experiencing of love.[16]

If the husband is the "head of his wife," and the wife is the "body of her husband," it is clear that they are one single subject, or as John Paul said, an "organic union."[17] Paul elsewhere states that husbands and wives ought to submit to one another "out of reverence for Christ."[18] Notice that the source of mutual subjection is reverence (piety) and its expression is love.[19] Paul is not talking about servitude, because love excludes any kind of submission that is servile.[20] It cannot be any form of submission that would degrade the individual, divide the couple, or contradict a true communion of persons.

So what kind of submission is ennobling? The only possible key to interpreting this passage is to understand the relationship between Christ and his bride, the Church.[21] This reveals the essential truth about marriage.[22] As the head of the Church, he is her savior, which means that he serves her by laying down his life as a sacrifice for her.

Saint Paul explains:

> And you, husbands, love your wives, as Christ loved the Church and gave himself for her, in order to make her holy by cleansing her with the washing of water accompanied by the word, so as to present his Church before himself all glorious, without spot or wrinkle or anything of the kind, but holy and immaculate.[23]

The model of love that Christ presents to husbands is one that is defined by giving "himself for her." As John Paul explained, this love is not simply an image, but a model of the love that a husband must show his wife in marriage.[24] Because it is a gift of self, Christ's love is faithful and permanent. So should be the love of a husband for his wife. When a man "gives" himself to a woman, this means not giving himself to other women in thought, word, or deed. He is hers.

But Christ's spousal love is also a redeeming love. John Paul pointed out that the essential goal of Christ's love is the sanctification of his bride.[25] The "great mystery" revealed by Christ's love for the Church shows that the spousal meaning of the body is linked with its redemptive meaning. In this link, John Paul noted that spouses find the answer to the question about the meaning of "being a body."[26]

In the above passage, Paul links the gift of the groom with the cleansing of the bride. She is made holy through "the washing of water accompanied by the word." Such language is foreign to modern readers, but would have been obvious to Paul's audience. In ancient Greek and Jewish cultures, the bride would take a "nuptial bath" prior to her wedding, with fragrant oils so that she would be as clean and beautiful as possible. Paul uses this as an image of baptism, which cleanses and beautifies the soul through the removal of sin and the infusion of grace.[27] The *Catechism* states, "The entire Christian life bears the mark of the spousal love of Christ and the Church. Already Baptism, the entry into the People of God, is a nuptial mystery; it is so to speak the nuptial bath which precedes the wedding feast, the Eucharist."[28]

After the nuptial bath, the bride is presented to the groom, and Paul uses her physical beauty as an image of spiritual beauty, which is holiness. John Paul explained that this "seems to indicate that moment of the wedding when the bride is led to the bridegroom already clothed in the wedding dress and adorned for the wedding."[29] He continued, "It is significant that *the image of the glorious Church* is presented, in the text quoted, *as a bride all beautiful in her body.* Certainly, this is a metaphor, but it is a very eloquent one and testifies how deeply important the body is in the analogy of spousal love."[30]

Paul continues:

> In the same way, husbands have the duty to love their wives as their own body, for the one who loves his wife loves himself. No one, in fact, ever hates his own flesh, but he nourishes and cares for it, as Christ does with the Church, because we are members of his body.[31]

If a husband is to nourish his wife as Christ cares for the Church, how does Christ nourish his bride? The nourishment that Jesus offers his Church is the Eucharist: "For my flesh is food indeed, and my blood is drink indeed."[32] Therefore, a husband's duty to love his wife can be summarized in the prayer of consecration at every Mass: "This is my body, given up for you." Not only do these words promise a sacrifice unto death, they also express a gift of life. They are the blueprint of spousal (and therefore, redeeming) love.

In the Eucharist, Christ becomes one flesh with his bride, the Church, in order to give her spiritual and eternal life: "He who eats my flesh and drinks my blood has eternal life."[33] Similarly, a husband gives his body to his bride so that she might receive the gift of life through their union.[34] Because the Eucharist is the spousal meaning of the body of Christ, it has a unitive and a life-giving dimension.[35] In fact, John Paul noted that "the Church too, united with Christ as the wife with her husband, draws from the sacrament of redemption her whole spiritual fruitfulness and motherhood."[36] This is why he called the Eucharist "*the Sacrament of the Bridegroom and of the Bride.*"[37]

When discussing the priesthood, John Paul noted that Jesus gave us the Eucharist to express in some way "the relationship between man and woman, between what is 'feminine' and what is 'masculine'"[38] Christopher West explained, "The spousal meaning of the man's body calls him to image God's initiation of the gift, whereas the spousal meaning of the woman's body calls her to image humanity's receptivity and response to the gift."[39] This template is repeated throughout Scripture, as can be seen when God initiates the covenants with Israel or when Christ initiates the laying down of his life for his bride. Similarly, man is called to initiate the gift of love for the woman. Although man's call to initiate love has become distorted by lust, his true mission remains.

If one understands God's plan for human love in marriage, not only does the meaning of the Mass become radiantly clear, all the sacraments take on a deeper meaning. John Paul noted that all the sacraments find their prototype in some way in marriage as the primordial sacrament.[40] In his words, marriage is "*the foundation of the whole sacramental order.*"[41] Each of them draw their significance and strength from Christ's spousal love.[42] Marriage illuminates every sacrament because we are uniting with Christ in a life-giving manner through our bodies.

Because human love within marriage is a sign that points humanity to God as the source of our ultimate fulfillment, Saint Paul continues in Ephesians 5 with the following statement:

> For this reason a man will leave his father and his mother and unite with his wife, and the two will form one flesh.[43]

As mentioned earlier, most people read this passage and never pause to consider: For what reason? The reason is to make visible the invisible love of God. Our creation as male and female, and the call of the two to become "one flesh" reveals a profound truth about Christ's relationship to us. As John Paul affirmed, it's the foundational way in which that eternal mystery of love becomes visible to us.[44] Put simply, the one-flesh union is a sign of God's love for humanity and of his plan of salvation.[45] This is not imposing theology onto sex, but revealing God's original design for human sexuality.

Unfortunately, because modern culture has degraded human sexuality, it is difficult for many to associate what is sacred with what is sexual. But the two are not meant to be in opposition. Karol Wojtyła devoted a significant portion of *Love and Responsibility* to the topic of sexology, and as Pope noted that while theology can illuminate the meaning of human sexuality, sexuality in itself can also reveal theological truths. In his words, "Purely 'biological' knowledge of the functions of the body as organism, connected with the masculinity and femininity of the human person, can help to discover the authentic spousal meaning of the body *only if it goes hand in hand with an adequate spiritual maturity of the human person*."[46] To reclaim the body and sexuality from a culture that has warped their meanings, what is needed is reverence, not fear.

Saint Paul culminates his remarks on marriage and the one-flesh union by declaring:

This mystery is great; I say this with reference to Christ and the Church.[47]

In the eyes of God, marriage is not primarily something two people *do* (exchange vows and then live together and love one another). Rather, marriage is primarily about what two people *become*: an image of Christ's love for the Church.[48] This is the "great mystery" that Paul is unveiling. What had been hidden as a mystery becomes visible as a sacrament.

The basic definition of a sacrament is a "visible sign of an invisible reality."[49] But the sacraments of the Church do more than signify spiritual realities. They are efficacious signs, meaning that they transmit grace. John Paul explained: "The sacraments infuse holiness into the terrain of man's humanity: they penetrate the soul and body, the femininity and masculinity of the personal subject, with the power of holiness."[50]

Therefore, John Paul declared that the sacrament of marriage "is a means for accomplishing in man the mystery hidden from eternity in God."[51] Do not gloss over the significance of these words: Marriage can accomplish in man the mystery hidden from eternity in God. The mystery hidden from eternity in God is his plan for the salvation of humanity, revealed in Christ.[52] Therefore, the identity—and mission—of Christian marriage is to be a manifestation of this. In the beginning, marriage was a clear sign of God's loving plan for humanity. Although this sign was tarnished through sin, Christ's love for his bride restores God's glorious plan.[53]

The light of this revealed analogy shines in both directions: Not only does the relationship between Christ and his Church reveal what marriage ought to look like, marriage also illuminates Christ's love for the Church.[54] For example, a husband and wife become one, and Jesus became one body with his Church by making a total gift of himself to her.[55] Thus, the bride of Christ is also called the body of Christ.

Because the Church is the body of Christ, she is the extension of the person of Jesus Christ throughout space and history. The two are one body, and therefore the Church has the power to sanctify souls, exorcise demons, forgive sins, proclaim truth infallibly, and turn bread into the flesh of God. To separate the redeeming power of Jesus Christ from his Church is not only a decapitation of the body of Christ, it is also a divorce. What God has joined, no one must separate.

After Paul declares the glory of God's plan for marriage, he concludes:

> Therefore also you, each one on his part, should love his wife as himself, and the woman should have reverence toward her husband.[56]

A helpful tool in biblical study is to remember that whenever you see the word "therefore," you should ask what it is "there for." In this case, Paul is proposing that the way spouses treat one another ought to be a result of the fact that they realize what they signify to the world. To love one another rightly, they must look at the love between Jesus and his bride. Or, in the words of John Paul, God is calling men and women to "*learn this sacrament anew* from the spousal relationship of Christ and the Church."[57] The two must be aware of the fact that their life and love together "carries *the sign of the mystery of creation and redemption*."[58] He added, "Spouses are therefore the permanent reminder to the Church of what happened on the Cross."[59]

To the degree that married couples absorb these truths, they will be all the more able to love one another. One of the functions of marriage is the sanctification of the spouses. As a result, faults will come to the surface and these sins and shortcomings will compel spouses to learn to forgive and seek forgiveness. Trials will arise that drive spouses to their knees in prayer. But these challenges do not erode love. They forge it.

# 5

# THE DIMENSION OF SIGN

**Language of the Body**

In the previous chapter of the Theology of the Body, John Paul examined the divine element of the sacrament of marriage (God's covenant and grace). Now, he turns his attention to its human dimension through which God acts (the sign).

If Christ's love for the Church is the model of the love between spouses, then their expressions of love are good to the extent that they mirror his love, becoming a clear sign of it. Therefore, when judging the morality of any sexual act, this is *the* question that must be considered: Am I expressing God's love with my body?[1]

God's love is free, total, faithful, and life-giving. However, modern sexuality is often an inversion of all this: Instead of being free, it is often paid for in prostitution, demanded in sexual abuse, and driven by addiction. Instead of being total, it is often reduced to "hookups," self-gratification, and empty encounters online. Instead of being faithful, it is often degraded by affairs both physical and fantasized. Instead of being fruitful, it is often contracepted, sterilized, and aborted.

The great sign that God created to be an image of his love for humanity has been systematically dismantled.

The task of the Christian is to reconstruct it so that the human body can again become the visible sign of God's invisible love. How is this possible?

By telling the truth with our bodies.

Because of its spousal meaning, the body is capable of expressing love. But it can also communicate the opposite. Because of this, John Paul spoke of the "language of the body." Not to be confused with "body language," which even animals can express through fear, aggression, or excitement, the body speaks the language of personhood; it speaks truth about our call to love like God. This is good news, not a dour list of moral regulations! In fact, Michael Waldstein points out that the Theology of the Body "is not primarily an admonition to follow the *law* of the body, but a persuasive proclamation of the *gospel* of the body."[2]

In John Paul's words, we can evaluate the morality of a sexual act by whether or not a couples' act possesses "*the character of a truthful sign*."[3] For example, during the sexual act within marriage, the bodies of the spouses speak the truth. The body is saying, "I am completely yours. I give myself to you." The total gift of the body corresponds with the total gift of the person. However, just as the body is capable of speaking the truth, it is also capable of lying. Sexual intimacy outside of marriage is one such example. The bodies are saying, "I am completely yours. I give myself to you." But in reality, no total gift of self is taking place.

Even though a dating couple might not intend to be deceitful in their relationship, sexual intimacy outside of marriage is a lie in the language of the body. It is not merely that sexual intimacy belongs *in* marriage, but that intercourse *is* marital. The words "I take you as my wife/as my husband" can only be fulfilled by sexual intercourse.[4] The wedding vows become flesh as the words pass on to the reality.

Although we are the authors of the language of the body, this does not mean we can make its meaning relative, determining for ourselves what is good and evil. The subjective expression should correspond with the objective reality.[5] This can be difficult, because John Paul noted that concupiscence brings about many errors in rereading the language of the body.[6] We're tempted to bend the truth, and this tendency does not end when one enters marriage.

Husbands and wives must be diligent in expressing the truth in and through their bodies. In fact, they have a special duty to do so. Because the body is capable of speaking a language, John Paul noted that husbands and wives are capable of offering a testimony worthy of true prophets.[7] A prophet is someone "who expresses with human words the truth that comes from God."[8] Their job, as a married couple, is to "proclaim exactly this 'language of the body,' reread in the truth."[9]

**Song of Songs**
After introducing the concept of the language of the

body, but before explaining how men and women can apply these teachings to their daily lives, John Paul prepared ten more reflections to discuss the Song of Songs, Tobit, and Ephesians. However, a significant portion of these talks were never delivered because he deemed them too delicate for younger listeners. It was not until many years later that the full texts became available to the public.

John Paul began with a reflection on the Song of Songs, which is a celebration of erotic love. The author's poetry weds the sacred and the sexual, as the words of the bride and bridegroom are interwoven like a duet.[10] Through it, John Paul leads the reader through a series of steps that show the maturation of the sacramental sign. Modern readers might wonder why sensual literature belongs in the middle of the Old Testament, but the Jews regarded it highly. The renowned first-century sage Rabbi Aqiba declared, "All the ages are not worth the day on which the Song of Songs was given to Israel; for all the Writings are holy, but the Song of Songs is the Holy of Holies."[11]

In John Paul's words, the Song of Songs is like taking Adam's first fascinated gasp at the sight of Eve and turning it into an entire book of poetry![12] In it, the couple expresses mutual admiration for one another in their masculinity and femininity. In particular, the groom expresses fascination and wonder for the bride's body, which reveals her as a person. He stands in amazement not only of her, but of the love they share. The bridegroom's eyes and heart are dominated by the revelation of femininity, and the gift that she is to him.[13] However, a warning is given that the man cannot consider her only as an object of erotic fascination. Rather, she is a person—a sister—created for her own sake.

Just as Christ desires his bride to be spotless and beautiful, so too does the groom in the Song of Songs, saying "*You are all-beautiful . . . and there is no spot in you.*"[14] This is not a superficial desire for physical attractiveness alone. Rather, the beauty of the body is a metaphor of holiness, which is the absence of the blemish of sin. One mark of authentic love is that one desires and works toward the good of the other. John Paul explained, "The good that the one who loves creates with his love in the beloved is like a test of that same love and its measure."[15] In other words, if a man claims to love a woman without safeguarding the beauty of her soul, his love is false.

However, his desire for beauty is a good thing. John Paul pointed out, "The male aspiration born from love on the basis of the 'language of the body' is a search for integral beauty, for purity free from every stain; it is a search for perfection that contains, I would say, *the synthesis of human beauty, beauty of soul and body.*"[16] More often than not, because of concupiscence, men and women often seek external beauty in the other (and in themselves) with little or no consideration of spiritual beauty. The solution to this, however, is not to disdain the goodness of the body, but to learn the language it is proclaiming. John Paul explained, "Both the femininity of the bride and the masculinity of the bridegroom speak without words."[17] The language of the body, expressed in desire, leads to the union of spouses, where they belong to one another.[18]

The key question posed by the Pope was this: Who will man be for woman, and who will woman be for man?[19] In the groom's admiration of the bride, he declares, "You have ravished my heart, my sister, my bride."[20] John Paul noted that this is a test of the motives of the man's heart.[21] Is he seeking love or lust? Is his interest self-gift or self-gratification?

The answer is provided by the groom, when he refers to her as "sister." While this might strike readers as awkward and unromantic, it refers to the fact that she is a sister with him in humanity, but is distinct in her femininity. Their difference, John Paul taught, is "not only with regard to sex, but to the very way of 'being a person.'"[22] For example, one of the distinct attributes of femininity is the woman's openness toward others. But this presents a question for the man. John Paul explained: "The 'sister' in some sense helps the man to define and conceive himself, she becomes, I would say, a challenge in this direction."[23]

The groom in the Song of Songs accepts this challenge, and continues to refer to her as a sister, and she responds, "Thus I am in his eyes as the one who has found peace!"[24] John Paul noted that the reason for her peace is that her groom reread the language of the body in truth and therefore discovered the inviolability of her as a person.[25] While this sounds complicated, it is not. She presented herself to the eyes of the man as the "master of her own mystery."[26] Because she is a person, no one can act on her behalf. She is free to make a gift of herself, and this freedom shows her dignity. He may not choose for her or impose his will upon her.

The groom is aware of this, as indicated by the way he speaks of her. He says, "*A garden closed* you are, my sister, bride, a garden closed, *a fountain sealed.*"[27] She is a gift to be received, not an object to be grasped. Because the bride is the "master of the intimate mystery of her own femininity," she alone can unveil the mystery and make the gift of herself.[28] On his part, the groom is required to have purity not only in his actions, but in his intentions, so as to respect her inviolability.

Because he is conscious that she is a gift, she freely gives herself and responds by saying, "I am my beloved's and my beloved is mine."[29] John Paul continued, "The bride knows that *'his desire' is for her*. She goes to meet him with the readiness of the gift of self. The love that unites them is of a spiritual and sensual nature together."[30] This demonstrates why a man cannot love a woman properly as a bride without first loving her as a sister.

After speaking about the woman being a garden locked and a fountain sealed, the love poetry progresses to what John Paul considered the closure and crowning of everything in the Song of Songs.[31] The bride declares, "Set me as a seal upon your heart, as a seal upon your arm; for love is strong as death."[32] John Paul exclaimed, "Here we reach in a certain sense the peak of a declaration of love."[33] She opens to him because he is ready to commit his entire life to her and love her unto death.

In light of this love story, it becomes clear that the Church's teachings on marriage are not arbitrary or imposed moral rules. Rather, they guard and proclaim the deepest cravings of the human heart: to make a gift of ourselves in imitation of the God who created us. When the language of the body is reread in the full truth of the person and love, it leads us to see that authentic love is strong as death.[34]

However, John Paul took his reflection one step deeper, saying, "These words express the power of love, the force of eros in loving union, but they also say (at least indirectly) that in the 'language of the body' this love finds its conclusive end in death."[35] Earthly love—no matter how intoxicating—is not the ultimate fulfillment of the human heart. He continued, "In the Song of Songs, human eros reveals the face of *love* ever *in search* and, as it were, *never satisfied*."[36] It is craving and restless. There is a need, John Paul argued, for eros to surpass itself.[37] But this kind of love would not be revealed until centuries after the Song of Songs had been written, when the apostle Paul speaks of a love that "will never end."[38]

**Tobit**

After discussing the Song of Songs, John Paul reflected on the marriage of Tobias and Sarah, from the book of Tobit. This too is an Old Testament love story about the relationship between a bride and groom whose love is stronger than death. In it, the archangel Raphael brings the two together, but they face a great obstacle to the future of their love: Sarah had been married seven times before, and each of her husbands was killed by a demon on the night of her wedding. Despite this, Tobias moves forward toward marriage with the encouragement of the archangel, and loved Sarah "to the point of no longer being able to draw his heart away from her."[39] Sarah likewise moved forward in faith, and John Paul noted, "Even if the demon's victim is to be Tobias alone, it is nevertheless easy to imagine what sacrifice of heart also Sarah would have had to undergo."[40]

Sarah's father wasn't nearly as optimistic as the two of them, and was digging the young man's grave on his wedding day![41] But he had not heard what the angel had spoken to Tobias, telling him what to do on the night of their wedding so as not to suffer the fate of the previous men she wedded. Raphael had said, "Then, before you unite yourself with her, first stand up, both of you, and pray. *Implore the Lord of heaven that his grace* and salvation *may come over you.* Do not be afraid; she was destined for you from eternity, and you are the one to save her. She will follow you, and I pledge my word she will give you children who will be like brothers to you. Do not worry."[42]

And so, on the night of their wedding, Tobias said to his bride, "Sister, get up. Let us pray and ask the Lord to give us his mercy." She rose with him in prayer for their protection, and he led her with the following petition:

Blessed are you, O God of our fathers, and blessed for all generations is your name. Let the heavens and the whole creation bless you for all ages. You created Adam, and you created his wife Eve to be a help and support for him. From the two of them the whole human race was born. You said, "It is not good that the man should be alone; let us make him a help similar to himself. Now it is not out of lust that I take this kinswoman of mine, but with right-ness of intention. Grant that she and I may find mercy and that we may grow old together." And they both said, "Amen, Amen."[43]

As in the Song of Songs, the groom refers to his bride as his sister, but he makes a remarkable statement in the prayer offered before consummating their union. Tobias tells God that he is not taking this sister of his because of lust, but with sincerity.[44] In all seventy-three books of the Bible, this is the only recorded prayer before a husband and wife become one flesh. In it, the groom testifies that his gift of self is sincere, and is not driven by lust. In saying this, Tobias is not implying that he lacks desire or attraction toward Sarah. Even the archangel Raphael acknowledges that she is beautiful![45] What Tobias is saying is that his passionate love for her is pure. John Paul noted that the fraternal character of their love is not eliminated, but rooted in spousal love.[46]

Like theirs, every marriage involves a great spiritual battle. As G.K. Chesterton remarked, "Marriage is an adventure, like going to war." Therefore, it is no coincidence that Saint Paul's proclamation of God's plan for human love in Ephesians 5 is followed by what John Paul called "a stupendous encouragement to spiritual battle" in Ephesians 6.[47] From the beginning, marriage is a life-or-death test. But John Paul reassured and reminded couples that love "is victorious because it prays."[48]

John Paul spent many decades working with young couples, and noted that young people often think that "conjugal union and life should bring them only happiness and joy. The experience of life shows that spouses are not seldom left disappointed in what they expected most."[49] With joy also comes tribulation. But the presence of crosses within marriage should not cause couples to despair. The Pope added, "The truth and strength of love show themselves in the ability to place oneself between the forces of good and of evil that fight within man and around him, because love is confident in the victory of good and is ready to do everything in order that good may conquer."[50]

Tobias and Sarah rely upon God to protect and bless their marriage, and John Paul noted that their prayer "becomes in some way the deepest *model of the liturgy,* whose word is *a word of power.* It is a word of power drawn from the sources of the covenant and of grace. It is the power that frees from evil and purifies."[51]

He notes that one can see through the couples in the Song of Songs and in the book of Tobit how the language of the body becomes the language of the liturgy.[52] Compare, for example, the words of Tobias with the vows of a wedding. Tobias says, "I take this kinswoman of mine. . . . Grant that she and I may find mercy."[53] John Paul noted, "The present liturgy of the Latin Church has the new spouses say, 'I take you as my wife/as my husband. . . . I promise to be true to you. . . . I will love you and honor you all the days of my life.'"[54] The marriage liturgy, then, is not a mere ritual to ratify a relationship. It's a sacramental expression of the call to self-giving love that God inscribed in the human body.

However, if the human body expresses the language of the liturgy, it also has the ability to invert it. For this reason, sexual intimacy is either an act of consecration or desecration. It can be sacramental or sacrilegious, liturgical or idolatrous.

### Ephesians
In his final reflection on the sign of marriage, John Paul returned for a concluding glance at the fifth chapter of Ephesians. As noted above, this is where Saint Paul speaks about marriage as a "great mystery" in reference to Christ and the Church. John Paul remarked,

"This text brings us to a dimension of the 'language of the body' that could be called 'mystical.'"[55] He added, "*The language and ritual* of the liturgy *are modeled after the 'language of the body.'*"[56]

To understand what he means here, it is necessary to realize he is now speaking of "liturgy" in a broader sense than the rituals of a wedding Mass. The *Catechism* defines "liturgy" as "the participation of the People of God in 'the work of God.'"[57] What is "the work of God"? It is the great mystery of redemption. Therefore, marriage, by its very nature, is liturgical. It is a participation in God's great plan of salvation.

What's remarkable about Saint Paul's teaching is not that Christ's love for the Church alone constitutes the "great mystery." Rather, John Paul noted that Saint Paul "does not hesitate to *extend that mystical analogy to the 'language of the body,'* reread in the truth of spousal love and of the conjugal union of the two."[58] Put simply, the sexual union of a husband and wife make visible the "great mystery" of God's great plan of salvation (the spousal union of Christ and the Church).

In fact, their whole married life together becomes a liturgical act as they make a gift of themselves to one another. These expressions of selfless love form the very heart and spirituality of marriage, lived out through the language of the body.[59] Together, they become "the visible sign of God's creative love."[60] When a husband and a wife realize this, they begin to experience the "reverence" that Paul mentions in Ephesians. John Paul described this awe as:

> . . . *a spiritually mature form* of that reciprocal *fascination,* that is to say, of the man for femininity and of the woman for masculinity, which reveals itself for the first time in Genesis 2:23–25. Later, the same fascination seems to run like a wide torrent through the verses of the Song of Songs to find, under wholly different circumstances, its concise and concentrated expression in Tobit. The spiritual maturity of this fascination is nothing but *the fruit born of the gift of fear,* one of the seven gifts of the Holy Spirit, which Saint Paul spoke about in 1 Thessalonians 4:4–7.[61]

To most, the word "fear" has only a negative meaning. Paul, however, is speaking about the profound sense of reverence a person experiences when he or she is in the presence of the sacred. For example, when the high priest entered into the Holy of Holies in the Old Testament, he did so with trembling reverence. He knew he was on holy ground. A similar reverent fascination is called for within the realm of sexual intimacy. This deep respect isn't merely a virtue. It is a gift of the Holy Spirit. When men and women experience this, John Paul noted that they will experience human love "in a depth, simplicity, and beauty hitherto altogether unknown."[62]

# HE GAVE THEM THE LAW OF LIFE AS THEIR INHERITANCE

**Understanding *Humanae Vitae***

The final chapter of the Theology of the Body is not a mere appendix or summary of what the Holy Father outlined in his series of audiences. It is the culmination of all of them. He noted, "The reflections about human love in the divine plan carried out so far would remain in some way incomplete if we did not try to see their concrete application in the area of conjugal and familial morality."[1] In particular, John Paul focused on the 1968 encyclical of Pope Paul VI, *Humanae Vitae,* on the regulation of birth. In this controversial letter, Pope Paul VI reaffirmed the historic Christian teaching against contraception, and explained why all sexual acts must remain ordered toward the procreation of human life.

Although this encyclical is the last topic addressed, it is the true focus of the Theology of the Body.[2] In fact, he noted that his whole teaching on the body is "*an extensive commentary* on the doctrine contained precisely in *Humanae Vitae.*"[3] This is not to say that the Theology of the Body is merely an elaborate argument against contraception, but that this key moral issue cannot be fully understood without grasping the redemption of the body and the sacramentality of marriage. The Holy Father felt so strongly about this topic that he declared that the teaching of *Humanae Vitae* is a "struggle for the value and meaning of humanity itself."[4]

Such language might strike some as extreme, but the Pope unhesitatingly affirmed that when it comes to this issue, man's identity is at stake. To understand why the Pope would say this, it is necessary to understand God's plan for life-giving love.

There are certainly times when husbands and wives have good reasons to postpone pregnancy. But to evaluate the morality of an action, one must not look only at motives and intentions, but also at objective standards.[5] Specifically, the use of contraception contradicts the nature of the sexual act, the promises made by the spouses, and the nature of the spouses themselves.

### Contradiction of the Sexual Act

First, contraception contradicts the nature of sexual intimacy, which has a unitive and procreative meaning that belong together. To understand why it is immoral to separate them, imagine if a husband wanted to use his wife for her procreative potential, but had no desire to unite with her on a personal level. To avoid any emotional entanglement, he looked away from her whenever they became physically intimate. His disordered and distorted use of the gift of sexuality is obvious. Contraception is a distortion of the sexual gift for the opposite reason. It seeks the physical and emotional sensation of the marital union while blocking its procreative potential.

In John Paul's words, the inseparability of the two meanings of the sexual act is nothing else than "rereading the 'language of the body' in the truth."[6] The body has a spousal meaning, and speaks a language of total self-giving. Contraception contradicts this meaning at its core. This is not about conforming to impersonal biological laws, but about conforming our wills to the personal Creator who designed our biology and imprinted his will into our human nature.[7]

Sadly, most people view *Humanae Vitae* as an outdated Vatican document, out of touch with the needs and challenges of modern couples. Standing against the Church, her opponents are painted as compassionate champions of a woman's right to have access to family planning as a form of health care. What these opponents never seem to ask is the underlying assumption of *Humanae Vitae*: What if the woman's body is already perfectly made? What if she doesn't need drugs, chemicals, and barriers to plan her family? What if she simply needs to be understood, and her fertility reverenced? If a couple can learn the woman's fertility, consider the outcome: Instead of controlling her body with chemicals and devices in order to conform to their sexual desires, the couple learns to control their sexual desires in order to conform to the perfect way that God has created their bodies. This is authentic sexual liberation. When viewed in this light, it's easier to see that the Church's teaching on family planning is not simply true and good, but is most of all beautiful.

Contraception might seem like an advancement for humanity because it allows mankind to rule over one's nature in a way that makes his or her life more convenient. However, John Paul noted that human progress and development can't be measured by technology alone, but by what truly promotes the good of man, ethics, and what is authentically humanistic.[8] Contraception has failed on all three of these counts. Once the sexual act was divorced from its link to procreation, all other distortions of sexuality became acceptable. Contraception allowed sex without commitment like never before, and led men to view women as objects rather than respected and beloved companions.[9] This is not human progress.

What many people overlook is that contraception was not invented to prevent the possibility of pregnancy. It was invented to prevent the need for abstinence. However, many problems arise when man seeks to master nature without mastering himself.

### Contradiction of Wedding Promises

Contraception is not immoral merely because it divides the two meanings of the marital act. In doing so, it is also a contradiction of the vows and promises that spouses make to one another on their wedding day. As part of the marriage liturgy, spouses promise to give themselves to one another and to welcome children into their lives. Because the sexual act is a renewal of the wedding vows, contraception is a contradiction of those promises.[10]

In becoming one flesh, the two not only renew their love for one another, they also become an icon of Christ's love for his bride, and her receptivity to his divine life. Contraception falsifies this sign. If couples are called to be a visible sign of God's creative love, then the deliberate sterilization of the sexual act is the inversion of their calling.[11]

### Contradiction of the Person

Finally, contraception is not merely a contradiction of the meaning of the sexual act and of the wedding promises made by spouses. It is contrary to the identity of the human person.[12] John Paul explained, "The human body in its masculinity and femininity is oriented from within to the communion of persons. . . . In this consists its spousal meaning."[13] In other words, contraception isn't immoral because it merely violates the nature of the sexual act, but because in doing so, it violates human nature itself.

Written into our humanity is an invitation to express sexual intimacy as persons made in God's image and likeness. This is why John Paul stated that God's law of life was given to man as a precious *inheritance*—

not a burdensome prohibition. When speaking to college students in Poland, he reminded them of the joy one should experience in discovering this, saying, "God who is Father, who is Creator, planted a reflection of his creative strength and power within man. . . . We should sing hymns of praise to God the Creator for this reflection of himself in us—and not only in our souls but also in our bodies."[14]

Through their life-giving love, spouses form an image of the Blessed Trinity on earth.[15] Although theirs is only a faint reflection of the glory of the communion that exists between the Father, Son, and Holy Spirit, it is their identity and therefore their mission to become who they are. Quoting Pascal Ide, Waldstein remarked that "one can condense the whole argument of the Theology of the Body in the statement 'Gift expresses the essential truth of the human body.'"[16]

If "gift" is who we are and what we are called to be, the language of contraception speaks the opposite. There is no true mutual gift of self or acceptance of one's self by the other. In John Paul's words, "Such a violation of the inner order of conjugal communion, a communion that plunges its roots into the very order of the person, *constitutes the essential evil of the contraceptive act.*"[17]

## The Center of Conjugal Spirituality

When spouses are aware of their identity, their calling becomes clear. In the words of John Paul, the Holy

Spirit stirs up within spouses an "attitude of *reverence for the work of God*."[18] This does not dampen the experience of intimacy between spouses, but safeguards it. The Pope pointed out that this reverence has enormous significance for the expressions of affection within marriage, "because it goes hand in hand with the capacity for profound pleasure in, admiration for, disinterested attention to the 'visible' and at the same time 'invisible' beauty of femininity and masculinity."[19]

Although most people don't associate the word "chastity" with intimacy, it is a prerequisite for it. As discussed earlier, it is necessary to establish a true communion of persons. Regarding chastity in marriage, John Paul declared that this virtue is "at the center of conjugal spirituality."[20] Chastity, and the attitude of reverence that guides it, shapes the spirituality of couples and grants them a desire to protect the dignity of the sexual act. This manifests itself not merely in the sexual union, but continually through the various ways in which spouses express their love.[21] After all, a true communion of persons within marriage isn't simply expressed through sexual intimacy, but through becoming one in mind and heart. This attention to the whole person creates true unity.[22]

When spouses live life "according to the Spirit," it gives them a deep awareness of the holiness of the life they have the capacity to create.[23] Contraception does the opposite because it displays a lack of reverence for God's work and a lack of awareness of the spousal meaning of the body.[24] Therefore, John Paul stated that this lack of understanding—connected with the contraceptive practices and mentality—is "the antithesis of conjugal spirituality."[25]

## Natural Family Planning

Many wonder, "If the Church is opposed to contraception, what are couples expected to do if they have a serious reason to avoid pregnancy?" The answer to this is Natural Family Planning, which allows couples to achieve or postpone pregnancy without the use of contraception. Instead of engaging in the sexual act and blocking its life-giving potential, couples who use NFP receive both the fertile and infertile times of their marriage as a gift. If they need to avoid or postpone pregnancy, they practice abstinence during the fertile times, and express love in nongenital ways. Through NFP, couples are able to plan their families while expressing reverence for God's gift of sexuality.

Some people assume that "good" Catholics use Natural Family Planning while "bad" Catholics use contraception. This attitude fails to recognize that the default position for all couples ought to be the realization that children are "the supreme gift of marriage."[26] Therefore, NFP ought to be used as a method of regulating conception when necessary, not of avoiding a family.[27] Responsible parenthood means more than avoiding children. Sometimes it means having more of them![28]

One reason why many couples do not use NFP is that it requires times of abstinence within marriage. Indeed, there are times when abstinence within marriage can be against God's plan. Saint Paul advises spouses: "Do not refuse one another except perhaps by agreement for a season, that you may devote yourselves to prayer; but then come together again, lest Satan tempt you through lack of self-control."[29]

Because the one-flesh union is the renewal of a sacrament and a manifestation of God's love, the devil desires to prevent or at least distort it. In fact, it could be argued that as desperately as the devil tries to get couples to become sexually intimate before marriage, to the same extent does he work to prevent them from becoming one flesh within the sacrament. Speaking of a married couple's unity in general, one priest noted, "Satan dares to approach only after he has isolated the man and the woman. When they are together, their bond is so profoundly and immediately rooted in the image of God that the devil cannot bear it. He isolates them from each other so that he may act."[30]

However, seasons of abstinence within marriage are necessary at times, and can be profound expressions of love. It's not simply that couples can express love in nonsexual ways during the infertile times, but that abstinence itself can be an expression of love because it is sometimes required in order to do what is best for the other. In fact, the inability to be abstinent within marriage reveals a lack of love.

The proper use of NFP is difficult, but with the help of God, the sacrifice is possible.[31] After all, the knowledge of a woman's fertility cycle alone does not create self-mastery.[32] John Paul pointed out that this "depends on the maturity of the inner man."[33] This process of maturation can be a difficult one, especially if the spouses did not practice chastity prior to marriage. The Church understands the challenge that this sometimes presents to spouses, but God's laws regarding the transmission of life do not contradict his call to love. Discovering God's plan for human love involves great sacrifice at times, but John Paul argued that "the *one and only true* good of the human person consists in putting this divine plan into practice."[34]

In the end, what is at stake is not whether or not the Church has a right to "be in the bedroom," as some complain. Rather, John Paul declared that the family and the call of men and women to life-giving communion is "at the center of the great struggle between good and evil, between life and death, between love and all that is opposed to love."[35]

### Living the Theology of the Body

Although portions of the Theology of the Body can be challenging to understand, the heart of its teaching is practical on every level of the Christian life.

For those who are unmarried, the Theology of the Body reveals that all persons are called to live out the spousal meaning of the body. One does not need to receive the sacrament of Holy Orders in order to make a gift of one's self through family life, service, intercessory prayer, fasting, work, and daily relationships and interactions. Nor is it necessary to enter marriage in order to foster authentic communion between persons. For example, true friendships can be formed rather than virtual ones that exist only through social media. Instead of having one's face perpetually immersed in the glow of a cell phone screen, a person can put it down during mealtime, family time, or even while interacting with an employee at a store.

Within dating relationships, the Theology of the Body reminds couples to speak the language of the body truthfully. By practicing chastity, they express reverence for the gift of their sexuality. They will discover that rather than inhibiting their freedom, this virtue makes them free to love. It will also free them to know if they are being loved, because chastity brings to light a person's intentions. For example, it has been said that what you win a person with is what you keep him (or her) with. If the other person is won over by the allure of pleasure, then the relationship will fade. After all, pleasure is repeatable; it can be obtained from any number of sources. However, the human person is unrepeatable. If you win a person with who you are, this gift cannot be repeated or replaced.

Regardless of one's vocation, every person is called to treat others as a gift and to make a gift of one's self. Even if a person is incapacitated and homebound, it is possible to make a gift of one's self through suffering. To do this, pray to God for the grace to love your crosses, and then offer your suffering as a prayer for others. Even in its brokenness, the human body remains a gift that can be offered for the glory of God. On his sixty-fifth birthday, John Paul wrote a personal prayer that offers the world a beautiful witness of how to do this. In it, he prayed:

> If one day illness touches my mind and clouds it, I do surrender to You even now, with this devotion that will later be continued in silent adoration. If, one day I were to lie down and remain unconscious for long, it is my desire that every hour that I am given to experience this be an uninterrupted thanksgiving, and that my ultimate breath be also a breath of love. Then, at such a moment, my soul, guided by the hand of Mary, will face You in order to sing Your glory forever. Amen.[36]

Some might argue that living out the Theology of the Body is a difficult task. But it could be argued that *not* living the Theology of the Body makes life only more difficult. How much simpler does life become when we realize that the purpose of life and the road map to heaven is stamped into our bodies as male and female? How much clearer does our path become when we realize that in becoming man, Jesus Christ not only revealed God to us—he revealed us to ourselves! Indeed, challenges will come, but with God's grace, John Paul promised that each person can live in "the hope of everyday."[37] One will achieve substantial victory not only over stubborn vices, but even within the deepest movements of the heart. The redemption of the body isn't just about heaven.

John Paul reminded the Church that to live the Theology of the Body, the three most important keys are prayer, the Eucharist, and confession.[38] Confession isn't simply the removal of the guilt of sin, but is an "increase of spiritual strength for the Christian battle."[39] In the Holy Father's prayer diary, he wrote, "The apostles of all times have drawn their strength to evangelize from frequent confession. Maybe this is why today there is a shortage of great apostles."[40]

Through the Eucharist, one can witness the Theology of the Body at every Mass, as Jesus becomes one flesh with his Church by offering his Body to his bride so that she might have eternal life. Rather than simply attending the Mass, the person who understands the Theology of the Body learns that the Mass is the model of Christian life: As Saint Paul exhorts his readers, "Present your bodies as a living sacrifice, holy and acceptable to God, which is your spiritual worship."[41]

Finally, through prayer, the Christian reciprocates God's gift of himself to each person. Prayer is not merely a means by which a person obtains the grace to live the Theology of the Body. Prayer itself ought to be a deep expression of it. In John Paul's words:

Prayer can progress, as a genuine dialogue of love, to the point of rendering the person wholly possessed by the divine Beloved, vibrating at the Spirit's touch, resting filially within the Father's heart. This is the lived experience of Christ's promise: "He who loves me will be loved by my Father, and I will love him and manifest myself to him" (John 14:21). It is a journey totally sustained by grace, which nonetheless demands an intense spiritual commitment and is no stranger to painful purifications (the "dark night"). But it leads, in various possible ways, to the ineffable joy experienced by the mystics as "nuptial union."[42]

When Christians grasp the beauty and power of the Theology of the Body, they will find within it the antidote to the culture of death, capable of triggering a new sexual revolution. The good news about God's plan for human love is too good to contain. It must be shared. On the following pages, you will find numerous resources and ministries for people of all ages to learn more about the Theology of the Body. Take advantage of these to deepen your ability to understand and share this message. Take up the challenge issued by John Paul, to persevere in learning the meaning of masculinity and femininity, not just intellectually, but in your heart.[43]

God's plan for human love does not require us to repress our desires or to pretend they don't exist, but to acknowledge their presence and their power, and to beg God for the strength to love as he loves. If we do this, and live out the call to love that is stamped into our bodies, our sexuality will not be something we hide from God. Rather, we will begin to see him in others—and even in ourselves. By making a gift of ourselves, God can shine through us onto those we love. And this is the greatest form of evangelization on earth: To make the invisible love of God visible by the way that men and women love.

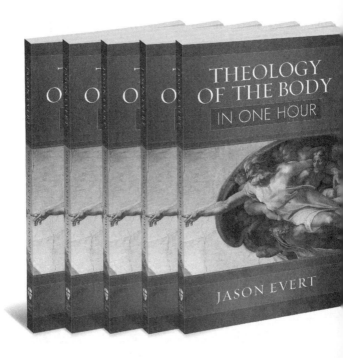

Obtain copies of this book
and others like it, for **$3 in bulk!**

To order, visit:

# Teach the Theology of the Body to Teens!

YOU: Life, Love, and the Theology of the Body (High school program)

Theology of the Body for Teens: Middle School edition

Theology of His Body / Theology of Her Body

To order these resources or donate to our ministry, please visit:

# Learn more about the Theology of the Body!

- **The Cor Project** is a global membership and outreach organization founded by Christopher West devoted to helping men and women learn, live, and share the Theology of the Body in compelling, life-transforming ways. Visit Corproject.com.

- **Dumb Ox Ministries** works with teens, young adults, and families; cultivating their authentic masculinity and femininity through the Theology of the Body, helping them to prepare for, discern, and pursue their unique vocations to love. Visit dumboxministries.com.

- **Into the Deep** provides outdoor Theology of the Body Retreats with Jen Messing. Visit idretreats.org.

- **JOYTOB** is the international teaching ministry of Damon Owens, offering Theology of the Body seminars, conferences, retreats, and parish missions. Visit joytob.org.

- **Pontifical John Paul II Institute for Studies on Marriage and Family** was established by Saint John Paul II as a theological center devoted to the study of the Church's teaching on marriage and the family. It offers accredited pontifical degree programs, as well as civilly accredited graduate degree programs (master's, license, and doctoral-level education). Visit johnpaulii.edu.

• **Ruah Woods** exists to restore the family and renew the culture by educating and training leaders and teachers to understand, embrace, and evangelize the message of Theology of the Body. Visit ruahwoods.org.

• **Tabor Life Institute** is dedicated to promoting the sacramental-liturgical worldview of the human person and the entire created order. Their mission is to help transform lives through the Theology of the Body. Visit taborlife.org.

• **Theology of the Body Evangelization Team (TOBET)** promotes the Theology of the Body through programs and resources designed for people of all ages. Visit tobet.org.

• **TheologyOfTheBody.net** offers audio and video presentations, books, articles, and other resources to learn about the Theology of the Body from a wide range of speakers and authors.

• **The Theology of the Body Institute** spreads the message of Theology of the Body through retreats, talks, graduate level courses, and clergy enrichment training for men and women of every vocation and walk of life. Visit TOBinstitute.org.

# ENDNOTES

## Preface

1 Peter 5:8.

2 Mieczysław Mokrzycki, World Youth Day Press Conference, Krakow, Poland, July 27, 2016.

3 Interview with Father Andrew Swietochowski, July 31, 2017.

4 The Pontifical Council for the Family and the International Institute of Studies on Marriage and Family.

5 Diane Montagna, "Online Exclusive: What John Paul II Intended to Say the Day He Was Shot," *Aleteia*, May 7, 2016.

6 Pope John Paul II, *Memory and Identity* (New York: Rizzoli, 2005), 164.

7 Pope John Paul II, Angelus message, May 29, 1994.

## Introduction

1 *Gaudium et Spes*, 36.

2 Other proposed titles included "Human Love in the Divine Plan" or "The Redemption of the Body and the Sacramentality of Marriage."

3 George Weigel, *Witness to Hope* (New York: Harper, 2001), 343.

4 Cf. *Catechism of the Catholic Church* 2516 (San Francisco: Ignatius Press, 1994).

5 Pope John Paul II, *Familiaris Consortio* 11 (Boston: Pauline Books & Media, 1981).

6 Mokrzycki, World Youth Day Press Conference.

7 George Weigel, *City of Saints* (New York: Image, 2015), 232.

8 Mokrzycki, World Youth Day Press Conference.

9 Pope John Paul II, *Master in the Faith* 2, Rome: December 14, 1990.

10 Matt. 19:8; Mark 10:6–9.

11 Matt. 5:28.

12 Matt. 22:30; Mark 12:25; Luke 20:35–36.

13 TOB 133:2.

14 Theology of the Body 15:1; 32:1, 3.

15 Cf. Pope John Paul II, *Man and Woman He Created Them: A Theology of the Body*, trans. Michael Waldstein (Boston: Pauline Books and Media, 2006).

16 TOB 23:5.

17 As quoted in Jean-Baptiste Chautard, *The Soul of the Apostolate* (Charlotte: TAN Books, 2012).

## Chapter 1: Christ Appeals to the "Beginning"

1 Cf. TOB 14:2.

2 Pope John Paul II, *Crossing the Threshold of Hope* (New York: Alfred A. Knopf, 1994), 121.

3 C.S. Lewis, *The Weight of Glory* (New York: Harper One, 2001), 31.

4 Address of His Holiness Pope Benedict XVI to the Participants in the Ecclesial Diocesan Convention of Rome, Basilica of St John Lateran, June 6, 2005.

5   TOB 14:4.

6   TOB 108:6.

7   Emphasis mine.

8   *Catechism of the Catholic Church*, 221; See also *Dominum et Vivificantem*, 10.

9   TOB 9:3.

10  Cf. *Witness to Hope*, 343.

11  Cf. TOB 21:3.

12  Pope John Paul II, *Gratissimam Sane*, 19.

13  Cf. TOB 66:1.

14  Cf. TOB 20:5.

15  Cf. TOB 14:4.

16  TOB 19:4; 96:6.

17  *Gratissimam Sane*, 19.

18  Cf. TOB 59:3.

19  Cf. TOB 14:6.

20  Christoph Cardinal Schönborn, preface, Pope John Paul II, *Man and Woman He Created Them*, xxiv–xxv.

21  TOB 18:4; cf. 13:3.

22  Pope Francis, *Amoris Laetitia*, 286.

23  Pope Francis, General Audience, April 15, 2015.

24  Cardinal Burke, *Hope for the World: To Unite All Things in Christ* (San Francisco: Ignatius Press, 2016), 102.

25  TOB 29:4.

26  TOB 28:4.

27  TOB 59:2.

28  *Gaudium et Spes*, 22.

29  TOB 19.

30  Cf. TOB 16:3; 19:5.

31  Cf. Wojtyła, *Love and Responsibility*, 41.

32  Cf. TOB 12:2.

33  TOB 13:1.

34  Cf. Michael Waldstein, *Theology of the Body Map* (Florida: Sapientia Press of Ave Maria University, 2017), 12.

35  TOB 13:1.

36  Louann Brizendine, *The Female Brain* (New York: Morgan Road Books, 2006), 77.

37  TOB 13:1.

38  Cf. TOB 19:5.

39  TOB 32:1; 15:1.

40  TOB 48:5.

41  Cf. TOB 15:5; 45:3.

42  *Gaudium et Spes*, 24.

43  Cf. TOB 130:5.

44  Cf. TOB 15:5.

45  Cf. TOB 15.

46  Cf. TOB 15:1; 46:6.

47  Cf. TOB 14.

48  Cf. TOB 75:1.

## Chapter 2: Christ Appeals to the Human Heart

1   TOB 43:7.

2   Cf. TOB 58:5.

3   *Catechism of the Catholic Church* 2336.

4   Cf. TOB 32:3.

5   Cf. TOB 45.

6   Cf. TOB 31:6.

7   Cf. TOB 26:4.

8   Pope John Paul II, *Crossing the Threshold of Hope*, 228.

9   TOB 26:4.

10  Pope John Paul II, *Jesus, Son and Savior* (Boston: Pauline Books & Media, 1996), 31.

11  Cf. Wojtyła, *Love and Responsibility*, 161–62.

12  Cf. TOB 28:3.

13  Cf. TOB 32:6.

14 Cf. TOB 32:5.

15 TOB 32:6.

16 Cf. TOB 31:3.

17 Cf. TOB 29:2.

18 Cf. TOB 29:5.

19 TOB 29:5.

20 TOB 27:4.

21 Cf. TOB 29:3.

22 TOB 29:2.

23 Cf. TOB 28:5.

24 Cf. Wojtyła, *Love and Responsibility*, 187.

25 Cf. TOB 12:1; cf. 28:6

26 Cf. Wojtyła, *Love and Responsibility*, 179.

27 Cf. TOB 12:1.

28 Cf. TOB 12:1.

29 Cf. TOB 16:2.

30 TOB 16:3.

31 Cf. TOB 46:5.

32 Cf. TOB 44:6.

33 TOB 45:5.

34 Cf. TOB 31:1.

35 Dr. Timothy Patitsas, "Chastity and Empathy: Eros, Agape, and the Mystery of the Twofold Anointing," *Road to Emmaus* 1, no. 60 (Winter 2015), 7.

36 Cf. TOB 49:5.

37 TOB 32:3.

38 Cf. TOB 32:3.

39 Cf. TOB 32:5.

40 Cf. TOB 39:4

41 *Mulieris Dignitatem*, 14.

42 Cf. TOB 48:3.

43 TOB 48:4.

44 Cf. TOB 49:7.

45 TOB 43:5.

46 TOB 43:6.

47 Cf. TOB 43:5.

48 Pope John Paul II, *Man and Woman He Created Them*, 225.

49 Christopher West, *Heaven's Song* (West Chester, Pa.: Ascension Press, 2008), 47.

50 Thomas Hüetlin *and* Claudia Voigt, "Sexologist Volkmar Sigusch: 'Our Society Is Still Ignorant about Sex,'" *Spiegel Online,* March 11, 2011.

51 TOB 40:4.

52 Cf. TOB 40:1.

53 Cf. TOB 40: 5.

54 Pope John Paul II, *Memory and Identity*, 29.

55 Pope John Paul II, *Man and Woman He Created Them*, 125.

56 TOB 47:2.

57 TOB 47:5.

58 Cf. TOB 101:3.

59 Cf. TOB 47:6.

60 TOB 48:1.

61 Cf. TOB 47:5.

62 TOB 128:3.

63 TOB 113:5.

64 Patitsas, "Chastity and Empathy," 10.

65 Ibid., 42.

66 Ibid., 7.

67 *Catechism of the Catholic Church* 2519.

68 TOB 57:3.

69 Wojtyła, *Love and Responsibility*, 190.

70 Pope John Paul II, *Memory and Identity*, 29.

71 Ibid., 30.

72 Cf. TOB 43.

73 Wojtyła, *Love and Responsibility*, 181.

74 Cf. TOB 132:5.

75 TOB 46.

76  TOB 46:4.

77  TOB 46:6.

78  TOB 46:2.

79  TOB 46:6.

80  Pope John Paul II, *Veritatis Splendor*, 103.

81  J. Brian Bransfield, *The Human Person* (Boston: Pauline Books & Media, 2010), 246.

82  Cf. Christopher West, *Theology of the Body Explained* (Boston: Pauline Books & Media, 2008), 212.

83  Cf. TOB 54:3, 58:7; 129:5.

84  *Veritatis Splendor,* 15.

85  TOB 58:6.

86  Cf. TOB 40:5.

87  Paul Thigpen, *A Dictionary of Quotes from the Saints* (Ann Arbor, Mich.: Charis Books, 2001), 28.

88  Cf. West, *Theology of the Body Explained*, 217.

89  TOB 17:6.

90  TOB 33:2.

91  TOB 33:2.

92  TOB 43:7.

93  Cf. TOB 41:1.

94  Talmud, Sota, III, 2; V, 7; Berakhot, 9, as mentioned in Father Alexander Men, *Son of Man* (Yonkers, N.Y.: St. Vladimir's Seminary Press, 1998), 93.

95  Cf. TOB 63.

96  TOB 63:4.

97  Cf. TOB 62:5.

98  Cf. Wojtyła, *Love and Responsibility*, 186–93.

99  Cf. TOB 63:2.

100 Cf. TOB 61:3.

101 TOB 61:3.

102 TOB 43:2.

103 Cf. TOB 43:2.

104 TOB 40:3.

105 Cf. TOB 42:4.

106 TOB 43:3.

107 Cf. TOB 39:5.

108 TOB 100:6.

109 Cf. Wojtyła, *Love and Responsibility*, 108.

110 Ibid., 106, 170–171.

111 Cf. TOB 56:1.

112 TOB 13:1.

113 TOB 49:7; Cf. 57:2–3.

114 Cf. Wojtyła, *Love and Responsibility*, 146.

115 Cf. TOB 129:1.

116 Cf. TOB 128:3.

117 TOB 49:6.

118 Pope John Paul II, *Man and Woman He Created Them*, 64.

119 TOB 48:5.

120 Cf. TOB 101:1.

121 Cf. TOB 15:4.

122 TOB 48:2.

123 TOB 48:3.

124 TOB 48:5.

125 TOB 58:7.

126 Cf. *Catechism of the Catholic Church* 2342.

127 Cf. TOB 56:1.

128 R.E. Guiley, *The Quotable Saint* (New York, NY: Checkmark Books, 2002), 274.

129 St. Augustine, *Conf.* 6,11, 20: PL 32, 729–730.

130 Cf. TOB 58:5.

131 TOB 51:5 footnote.

132 TOB 45:4; Cf. 55:7.

133 TOB 58.7.

134 Cf. TOB 101:5.

135 TOB 58:6.

136 Cf. TOB 24:3.

137 Cf. *Catechism of the Catholic Church* 1775.

138 Cf. TOB 58:5.

139 TOB 58:7.

140 1 Thess. 4:4; Cf. TOB 54:5.

141 Cf. TOB 57:2, 101:5.

142 TOB 54:4.

143 1 Cor 6:19 (RSVCE).

144 Cf. TOB 56:4.

145 TOB 19:2.

## Chapter 3: Christ Appeals to the Resurrection

1   Cf. TOB 66:2.

2   Peter Kreeft, *Everything You Ever Wanted to Know About Heaven* (San Francisco: Ignatius, 1990), 93.

3   Cf. TOB 67:1.

4   Cf. TOB 66:6.

5   Cf. TOB 67:2.

6   TOB 75:1.

7   Cf. TOB 68:3.

8   TOB 67:5.

9   TOB 68:4.

10  TOB 67:3.

11  TOB 67:3.

12  Cf. TOB 67:3.

13  TOB 74:4.

14  As quoted in Jean-Pierre Batut, "The Chastity of Jesus and the 'Refusal to Grasp,'" *Communio (International Catholic Review)* 24 (Spring 1997): 13.

15  TOB 21:2.

16  Cf. TOB 80:1; 78:5.

17  Cf. TOB 81:2.

18  Cf. TOB 73.

19  Cf. TOB 76:6.

## Chapter 4: The Dimension of Covenant and Grace

1   Cf. TOB 101:7.

2   TOB 97:1.

3   TOB 93:2.

4   Cf. Hosea; Isaiah 54.

5   Cf. TOB 104:3.

6   Cf. Hosea 2:19–20.

7   Cf. John 3:29; Eph: 5:25–27; Rev. 19:9.

8   Cf. 96:6–7.

9   *Catechism of the Catholic Church* 1642.

10  Cf. TOB 95:7.

11  Cf. TOB 87:3; 104:1.

12  Eph. 5:22–24.

13  Cf. Ex. 18:4; Ps. 33:20.

14  Cf. TOB 12:3.

15  *Mulieris Dignitatem*, 10.

16  Cf. TOB 92:6.

17  Eph. 5:22–33; TOB 91:2.

18  Eph. 5:21 (RSCVE).

19  Cf. TOB 89:3.

20  Cf. TOB 89:4.

21  Cf. TOB 89:8.

22  Cf. TOB 90:2.

23  Eph. 5:25–27.

24  Cf. TOB 91:4.

25  Cf. TOB 91:6.

26  TOB 102:5.

27  Cf. TOB 91:8.

28  *Catechism of the Catholic Church* 1617.

29  TOB 91:8.

30  TOB 92:2.

31  Eph. 5:28–30.

32  John 6:55 (RSVCE).

33  John 6:54 (RSVCE).

34  Cf. TOB 92:8.

35  Cf. TOB 97.

36  TOB 97:4.

37 *Mulieris Dignitatem*, 26.

38 *Mulieris Dignitatem*, 26.

39 West, *Theology of the Body Explained*, 411; cf. *Mulieris Dignitatem* 4; TOB 92:6.

40 Cf. TOB 98:2.

41 TOB 95b:7.

42 Cf. TOB 99:1.

43 Eph. 5:31.

44 Cf. TOB 95b:6.

45 Cf. TOB 92:3, 93:2.

46 TOB 59:4.

47 Eph. 5:32.

48 Cf. TOB 103:3.

49 TOB 87:5.

50 TOB 117b:2.

51 TOB 93:5.

52 Cf. TOB 93.

53 Cf. TOB 98:8.

54 Cf. TOB 90; 93.

55 Cf. Eph 5:25; TOB 90:5.

56 Eph. 5:33.

57 TOB 102:2.

58 TOB 131:4.

59 *Familiaris Consortio*, 13.

**Chapter 5: The Dimension of Sign**

1 Cf. *Man and Woman He Created Them*, 122.

2 Ibid., 127.

3 TOB 37:6.

4 Cf. TOB 103:2.

5 Cf. TOB 104:7; 105:2,6; 107:5.

6 Cf. TOB 107:3.

7 Cf. TOB 104:1; 105:2; 106:4.

8 TOB 105:2.

9 105:2; cf. 104:8.

10 Cf. TOB 108:5.

11 Herbert Danby, *The Mishnah* (Peabody, Mass.: Hendrickson Publishers, 2011), 782.

12 Cf. TOB 108:5.

13 Cf. TOB 111:2.

14 TOB 108:8; Eph. 1:3–7, 10; Song 4:7; cf. TOB 112.3.

15 TOB 92:4.

16 TOB 112:3.

17 TOB 109:1.

18 Cf. TOB 112:5.

19 Cf. TOB 43:7.

20 Songs 4:9.

21 Cf. TOB 109:4.

22 TOB 109:4.

23 TOB 109:4.

24 Song 8:10; 109:4; Cf. 110:2.

25 Cf. TOB 110:8.

26 TOB 110:7.

27 Song 4:12.

28 TOB 111:6.

29 TOB 110:8; Song 2:16, 6:3.

30 TOB 111:5.

31 Cf. TOB 111:6.

32 Song 8:6.

33 TOB 111:6.

34 Cf. TOB 113:3.

35 TOB 112:5.

36 TOB 112:4.

37 Cf. TOB 113:2.

38 1 Cor. 13:4–8.

39 Tob. 6:19.

40 TOB 115:1.

41 Cf. Tob. 8:9.

42 Tobit 6:18.

43 Tobit 8:5–8.

44 Cf. Tob. 8:7 (RSVCE).

45 Cf. Tob. 6:12.

46 Cf. TOB 117.

47 TOB 88:5.

48 TOB 115:3.

49 TOB 83:3.

50 TOB 115:2.

51  TOB 115:6.

52  Cf. TOB 116:4.

53  Tob. 8:7.

54  TOB 117:3.

55  TOB 117b.

56  TOB 117:6.

57  *Catechism of the Catholic Church* 1069.

58  TOB 117b:1.

59  Cf. TOB 117b:3.

60  TOB 117b:3.

61  TOB 117b:4.

62  TOB 117b:5.

## Chapter 6: He Gave Them the Law of Life as Their Inheritance

1   TOB 118:1.

2   Cf. TOB 129; TOB 133.

3   TOB 133:2.

4   Pope John Paul II, *Crossing the Threshold of Hope*, 113.

5   Cf. TOB 121:1.

6   TOB 118:6.

7   Cf. TOB 124:6; West, *Theology of the Body Explained*, 591.

8   Cf. TOB 129:2; 133:3.

9   *Humanae Vitae*, 17; cf. Mary Eberstadt, *Adam and Eve after the Pill* (San Francisco: Ignatius Press, 2012).

10  Cf. TOB 118:4.

11  TOB 117b:3.

12  Cf. TOB 118:5; 123:7; 129.

13  TOB 130:5.

14  Karol Wojtyła, *The Way to Christ* (San Francisco: Harper, 1982), 55–56.

15  Cf. TOB 10:3.

16  Pope John Paul II, *Man and Woman He Created Them*, 124.

17  TOB 124:7.

18  TOB 132:4.

19  TOB 132:4.

20  TOB 131:2.

21  Cf. TOB 132:4.

22  Cf. TOB 132:5.

23  Cf. TOB 101:6.

24  Cf. TOB 132:1–2.

25  TOB 132:2.

26  Second Vatican Council, *Pastoral Constitution on the Church in the World of Today*, no. 50: AAS 58 (1966), 1070–72 [TPS XI, 292–93].

27  Cf. Wojtyła, *Love and Responsibility*, 242.

28  Cf. TOB 121:5.

29  1 Cor. 7:5 (RSVCE).

30  J. Brian Bransfield, *The Human Person*, 126.

31  Cf. *Humanae Vitae*, 20.

32  Cf. TOB 130:4.

33  TOB 130:4.

34  TOB 120:6.

35  Pope John Paul II, *Gratissimam Sane*, 23.

36  John Paul II's prayer written at Mechelen on his sixty-fifth birthday, May 18, 1985.

37  TOB 86:6, 7.

38  Cf. TOB 126:5.

39  *Catechism of the Catholic Church* 1496.

40  Pope John Paul II, *In God's Hands* (London: Harper One, 2017), 180.

41  Rom. 12:1 (RSVCE).

42  Pope John Paul II, *Novo Millennio Ineunte*, 33.

43  Cf. TOB 48:4.